# SYBIL THORNDIKE

# SYBIL THORNDIKE

## A Life in the Theatre

# Sheridan Morley

Preface by Sir John Gielgud

Weidenfeld & Nicolson · London

*For Juliet*
*who never knew her*
*and for the rest of us*
*who did*

# Contents

# Preface by Sir John Gielgud

In 1922 she came to the RADA and rehearsed my class in scenes from *Medea*. She had sandy hair in those days, arranged, if I remember rightly, in coils round her ears like radio-receivers, and wore long straight dresses in bright colours with strings of beads round her neck. She told me that Jason was a self-righteous prig and I must play him so. She exuded vitality, enthusiasm, generosity, and we were all spellbound as we listened to her.

I do not remember seeing her on the stage until *Saint Joan* in 1924, when I was lucky enough to be at the opening night, sitting with my parents in the dress circle of the New Theatre. It was an inspiring occasion – play, production, décor, acting, it all seemed perfect to me – and, at the end of the evening, when Sybil Thorndike led on the weary actors to take a dozen calls, all suddenly looking utterly exhausted by the strain of the long performance, I realized, perhaps for the first time, something of the agonies and triumphs of theatrical achievement.

I never saw her at the Vic in her Shakespeare seasons there, nor in Grand Guignol, in which she made so many successes, nor in *The Cenci*, but I do remember her in a Russian melodrama with Charles Laughton – sables and histrionics – and in *Cymbeline* as Imogen, in which I did not admire her greatly. Her Lady Macbeth (in a somewhat ill-fated production) was, I thought, fine, as was her Hecuba, and her Katharine in *Henry VIII*, but, for all her great gifts in costume plays, verse drama and bravura parts, I loved her best in modern work, when her own glorious humanity seemed to burn so brightly, plays like *Jane Clegg*, *The Corn is Green*, *The Distaff Side*, *The Linden Tree*, *Waters of the Moon*, *A Day by the Sea* in which it was such a delight for me to act with her for nearly a year.

Honesty and dedication shone from her. Her capacity for being interested in everyone and everything – politics, music, books, people, foreign languages, she found time for them all. Personal notes and letters – no typed achnowledgements from *her*. She had goodness in its rarest and noblest sense – faith and loving kindness and no pious nonsense – she

9

would suddenly surprise you by giving some quite sharply derogatory opinion or criticism, delivered without a hint of malice.

During these last years, it was sad to see her the victim of continual pain. But how magnificently she rose above it. 'My piffling arthritis,' she would say. With what unforgettably dignified simplicity she walked, leading her family, up the long nave of the Abbey at the memorial service for her husband, Lewis Casson, her head wrapped in the plain white silk scarf she always wore. How eagerly she followed every moment of the service, and how like her to wait afterwards to greet a great crowd of friends.

One day I called on her to find her sitting in an armchair reading Sir Thomas More, and on another when she was lying in bed evidently in great pain: 'A bit tired today,' she said, 'for it was Lewis's anniversary yesterday, so I got them to drive me up to Golder's Green and sat there for half an hour.' But she announced defiantly that she intended to come to see *No Man's Land* the following Friday. I begged her not to make the effort and thought no more about it, but when the evening came, sure enough during the interval, I heard over the loudspeaker above the chatter of the audience, her voice, unmistakably clear: 'Do you know my daughter-in-law, Patricia?' Ralph Richardson bounded into my dressing-room: 'She's here after all.' And of course we both had letters afterwards. George Devine told me that she came to see every one of the new plays when he was presenting them at the Court and would always write him vivid and constructive criticism as soon as she got home.

How fitting that her very last public appearance should have been at the Old Vic on its farewell night when, at the end of the performance, she was wheeled down the aisle in her chair to smile and wave for the last time in the theatre she loved so well.

Lively and personal, passionate and argumentative, always practising her piano, cooking her dinner, making her bed, travelling, acting, learning a new language or a new poem, simple clothes, simple tastes, a magnificent wife and mother – surely one of the rarest women of our time.

# The Old Lady Shows Her Medals

'A star not only of the stage, but of life'; so said A. P. Herbert in 1954, at a time when Sybil Thorndike had already turned seventy and was celebrating her fiftieth anniversary on the stage. After her death, more than twenty years later at the age of ninety-three, Herbert's feelings were echoed by Sir John Gielgud who, speaking at her memorial service, described Dame Sybil as 'the most greatly loved and admired English actress since Ellen Terry'.

Both women belonged to great if uneven and sometimes stormy stage partnerships, and there was one other link which went beyond their long friendships with each other and with Shaw: when Dame Sybil died in June 1976 they buried her in Westminster Abbey – a rare honour for a player, even a player queen, and one which had last been accorded to Dame Ellen's partner, Henry Irving, in 1905. Seven decades later, it seemed only right that the distinction should fall next to the actress who across half a century had been the first lady of the English theatre.

There have been two family biographies of Sybil Thorndike: the first was published by her brother Russell in 1929, and the second by her son John in 1972. What follows is not an outsider's unnecessary attempt at a third; rather is it a critical and photographic chronicle of one of the longest and most remarkable theatrical careers ever established, related wherever possible to Dame Sybil's own descriptions of her life and work. She did not, alas, leave behind an autobiography; but she did leave the tapes and transcripts of several long interviews given over the years to countless radio, television and print journalists including this one, and on these I have drawn as much as on her letters and the reports of those contemporary critics from Agate to Tynan who followed her marathon career with approbation, enthusiasm, amazement and sometimes also with despair and dismay.

Sybil Thorndike was nothing if not relentless: her interests over half a century of marriage, seventy years of acting and ninety years of life had little to do with money, good living, critical acceptance or advancement into high society. Instead, whether explaining the plot of *Medea* to miners' wives in the wartime Welsh valleys or urging the social and socialist reforms that she and her devoted husband Lewis Casson so resolutely believed in ('an actress has a stake in the country – she must stand up and be counted'), or debating with their beloved Bernard Shaw about what Joan had really been like, her life was one long celebration – religious and secular – of the human and theatrical spirit.

But neither her life nor her marriage was always or altogether easy: 'Lewis and I are very violent people', she once told a somewhat surprised Enid Bagnold, and on another occasion she added, 'Lewis and I had raging arguments all the time. I was jealous, too, of his occasional involvements with other women, although they generally became and remained good friends of mine. Of course I sometimes got slightly involved myself, but Lewis wasn't possessive … we were far too close for that. Infidelity depresses me terribly. But it wasn't really that with us. I suppose it was a sort of overflow of vitality.'

That vitality, together with a deep love for the dangerous unpredictability of the theatre ('films are far too safe'), was what kept her going, and from the summer of 1904 when, plump, innocent and already desperately over-enthusiastic, she set off to tour America with her teacher Ben Greet, across fully seventy more years she remained a human definition of what the theatre theatrical was all about.

'You had to shelter sometimes', said her son John Casson, 'from the bright sun of Sybil's enthusiasms, for fear that it would burn you', but audiences the world over were exposed frequently and regularly to the rays of a talent which could encompass Shaw and Shakespeare, Coward and Priestley, Euripides and Emlyn Williams. Often 'unfashionable' in terms of changing critical tastes, Sybil Thorndike was yet constantly beloved of her own public – not always the experienced West End public, but people all over the world for whom she would appear in a vast range of classical and modern work; people who perhaps didn't get the chance to go to the theatre a great deal and to whom she represented an 'other world' of tremendous grandeur: not grandeur of class or dress, necessarily, but grandeur of manner and gesture.

Hers was a career and a talent I'd known about all my life, but I first met her while I was an undergraduate at Oxford in 1961. I went backstage to interview her for a student paper after a curiously terrible first night – a wet Monday on the road and Dame Sybil (not for the first time, or

Sybil Thorndike as Mrs Tate in *Return Ticket*, Duchess Theatre, March 1965

indeed the last) in a shaky play with an uneasy supporting cast. I went through the stage door expecting, I think, to meet a rather depressed old lady; instead, there was this immensely jolly, buoyant little woman saying: 'Wasn't that terrible? Never mind, dear; they're a good company and we're all going to work jolly hard tomorrow and by the end of the week it'll be all right. He's a splendid playwright; do let's get on, and not worry about tonight.' I thought then, and often afterwards, that she was actually at her best in bad plays. I can't think of any actress I've ever seen rescue quite so many of them, often by holding them by the scruff of the neck and shaking hard. She invariably made you think that there was something in each one worth watching. Which of course was true: she was there.

From then onwards I was lucky enough to review or interview her almost every year until her death in 1976. At her flat in Chelsea, six weeks before the end, I asked if there was any part she still wanted to have a go at (since she was even then recording radio scripts from the bedside). 'I've played everyone I've ever wanted to', was the reply, 'except Queen Elizabeth, who I only played in one or two very short pieces. I always wanted to play a really big Elizabeth. Why? Because I adored her, I loved her; she was such an old bitch.'

Sybil's family always said that she viewed life as some vast Sunday-school outing on which everyone was supposed to be if not happy then at the very least tremendously jolly. From her earliest days at the Old Vic with Lilian Baylis in 1914, through to the night more than sixty years later, when she made her last public appearance in that same theatre, when the National bade farewell to the Vic, Sybil herself was ferociously jolly. The fire – and sometimes indeed the rage – of her love for Lewis and the stage, and a rampaging appetite for life, carried her through the vicissitudes of a career which often resembled nothing so much as a sustained if underplanned Royal tour.

Asked once how she had survived for so long she answered 'argument, energy, enthusiasm' and that was more or less that; the theatre was for her not a form of escape from reality but instead a workshop, a battle-ground and a church; and the theatre – Sybil's theatre – is inevitably what this book is all about. 'Acting', said John Casson, 'was for my mother a sort of evangelical banner under which to unite the rich, the poor, the educated, the ignorant, the long, the short and the tall.'

But the greatness of Sybil Thorndike, erratic though that greatness may sometimes have been, was not mirrored solely in the footlights: at political rallies, Indian independence conferences, suffragette meetings and pacifist demonstrations the world over, that well-known voice would ring out demanding justice, freedom, humanity or just a decent audience for the matinée. Her whole life was to do with greatness of heart, and if I think of her suddenly now it is not in a particular play or film, nor even reminiscing in her armchair at that famous flat in Swan Court, but rather backstage at the Savoy Theatre where one afternoon in 1974 she and my then six-year-old son were waiting side by side to make fleeting appearances in a *This Is Your Life* recording. Nearly ninety years separated the two of them, and what on earth they found to talk about I have somehow never thought to ask. But talk they did, and I know now that as long as he lives my son will never forget the almost magical impression she made. Come to think of it, nor will the rest of us.

# Rochester to the New World

To begin at the very beginning, Agnes Sybil Thorndike was born on 24 October 1882 at Gainsborough in Lincolnshire. Like Olivier, she was a clergyman's child: the family was sturdy but eccentric, according to her brother Russell, and largely tied up with the army and navy until their father went into the church. Sybil was the eldest of the four children of the Rev. Arthur Thorndike and his wife Agnes Bowers. Russell was the second, then Eileen and lastly Frank, all of whom went into the theatre for some time, as, later, did all four of Sybil's own children and many of the grandchildren. Sybil was the only one to be born in Gainsborough; before she was two her father was appointed a minor canon of Rochester Cathedral and the family moved to Kent where they stayed throughout the rest of her childhood.

The year 1882 also saw the birth of Virginia Woolf, James Joyce, Franklin Roosevelt and Samuel Goldwyn. In the theatre, however, those of her generation who were to join Sybil near the top of her profession and survive with her into the 1970s were in fact born six or seven years later (Edith Evans and Gladys Cooper in 1888, Cathleen Nesbitt in 1889, Zena Dare in 1887). In theatrical history the year of Sybil's birth was also distinguished by the stage début of Lillie Langtry and the founding of the first London school of dramatic art, under the auspices of such stars of the time as J. L. Toole and Mrs Kendal. It was also the year in which a Mr Samuel French began to publish plays.

The Rochester of Sybil's early years was then still Charles Dickens's Rochester despite the fact that he had died at his nearby Gadshill in 1870. Sybil and Russell thought he must have been Satan incarnate, since 'what the devil' and 'what the dickens' were interchangeable expressions of the time, but they were gradually disabused of that notion by proud neighbours who would show the children local landmarks from *Great Expectations* and especially *Edwin Drood*, since the latter book included Septimus Crisparkle, also a minor canon of Rochester.

There and then, perhaps, Russell began to develop the novelist's imagination which would one day lead him to the gothic thrills of *Dr Syn*; but for the time being, then as later, it was the theatre which primarily intrigued him and his sister. Plays would be performed on the nursery table of the house in Minor Canon Row until their nurse refused to serve tea 'off a place where people's boots have been', after which they took to performing on a bookshelf laid precariously across the bed in the spare room.

Both children were ruthless in their pursuit of amateur theatricals: having on another occasion found a store-room in which to act, but irked by the fact that a large number of loaves were stored there for the feeding of the needy on Sundays, Sybil laid out a mousetrap, caught a mouse, closed it in the store-room so that it demolished the loaves, and thereby ensured that for the following week the bread would be stored elsewhere and the store-room free for her performance.

By the time she was four, Sybil had made her amateur début in a performance for family and friends; by the time she was seven, she and Russell had done *The Dentist's Cure*, a harrowing drama conceived by themselves and subtitled *Saw their Silly Heads off* after *Sweeney Todd* – the beginnings, perhaps, of a fascination with Grand Guignol which was eventually to lead Sybil to her seasons at the Little Theatre in the early 1920s; by the time she was ten, the two of them were not only staging frequent and lengthy dramas around the house but also celebrating mock communions with cough mixture in the 'chalices' which were really silver rowing cups won by their father and now on unofficial loan from him.

The atmosphere in Minor Canon Row was thus almost overpoweringly religious-theatrical; three-quarters of a century later, in a BBC television conversation with the director Michael MacOwan, Sybil recalled:

I never went more than two months without being in a play from the time I was four. I was a mad keen amateur ... when Eileen was born we roped her in, and then Frank was born and he was roped in too. We roped them all in, but Russell and I played all the best parts ... our parents were Ellen Terry and Irving fans, and the first Shakespeare I remember was father reading *Hamlet* to me from having seen the Terrys. We always used to think that father, in the pulpit, looked like Forbes Robertson ... he had the most tremendous long breath, only beaten by Larry Olivier. Father could do the general exhortation 'Dearly beloved brethren, the scripture moveth us' one and a half times through in one breath; Larry could do it twice. We used to notice father in church, Russell used to nudge me and say 'Father's doing the collect all in one breath.' We were tremendously united in all our main interests and, of course, religion-mad. Father always encouraged us, from small children, to argue at our luncheon table, our supper table – we were always arguing. When father came home from church, on a Sunday morning after his sermon, we tore him to shreds. We've always been interested in religion, and when people talk about religion and put on holy faces we can't understand that, because father was never like that. I worshipped my father, I thought he was practically God and he was perfect. And I noticed that he always had poetry on his dressing table when he was shaving. He learned something every day and I thought 'What father does, I do.' I've always kept it up.

Around the time of Sybil's tenth birthday, her father was offered the living of the nearby St Margaret's parish and the family moved from Minor Canon Row to more spacious vicarage quarters. By now there was little doubt that Sybil would be going into public performance of one kind or another, although at that stage it might well have been musical rather than dramatic since her mother played the piano and was an excellent organist as well. Vicarage life was a comfortable one (Sybil's mother had once met Oscar Wilde and was much admired locally for the use she had made of his hints on how to create 'the house beautiful'), and Sybil was now old enough to start at the girls' grammar school on the Maidstone Road in Rochester where she played a memorable Brutus costumed accurately but for a curious curly dagger: 'I suppose', said Russell scathingly afterwards, 'Brutus was given that by Othello for a christening present?' Russell himself was now away at St George's in Windsor during term time, and as the younger children were still not old enough to take his place in the family plays, Sybil's thoughts began to turn more and more toward the piano. She played 'Men of Harlech' and 'The British Grenadiers' on drill days and helped out on the piano at the Sunday school where she'd been a leading light since the age of ten.

Upbraided by both her father and her headmistress for being lazy in school, Sybil decided to start taking her piano lessons very seriously indeed, spurred on by the promise of a London concert. It was to be held at Steinway Hall and on the great day, uncharacteristically, her nerves got the better of her:

I really thought I'd die. And that lovely man Hayden Coffin was on the same programme, and he caught hold of me and said 'Little girl, you mustn't be nervous like this. Come up with me.' And he said 'Look at that old man in the front row, now you play to him, and go and just play to him' and that suddenly bucked me up. Funny little podge me, on I walked in white nun's veiling, with brown stockings and shoes; I played Beethoven and was encored – oh! but the nerves ... no child of eleven ought to be nervous like that.

Terrified though she'd been, Sybil had nonetheless reached a wider audience than the family and friends at Rochester and she was still not twelve. Within another eighteen months she was having regular weekly piano lessons at the Guildhall, though the theatre was not altogether forgotten. Russell recounts an outing to their first real stage show which was *The Private Secretary* at the Chatham Opera House:

We had no idea that anything could be so funny in this world. Sybil rather spoilt my pleasure by getting the most awful attack of hiccoughs, because she couldn't stop laughing. She made me embarrassed. She laughed and hiccoughed at the same time. And so loud. An old man sitting the other side of father remarked ''Pon my word, I've enjoyed watching that young woman more than the play.' I thought it was a pity that Sybil couldn't have enjoyed herself without getting hiccoughs so loud, but she never had any restraint even in those days. I felt she had entirely forgotten father's injunction to remember that she was a Thorndike and a lady. I laughed too, but I did it in a more decent manner. Sybil is always just a little too boisterous.

Her own equally boisterous grammar-school rendering of Brutus had encouraged her father to subscribe to the Henry Irving Shakespeare set which arrived in Rochester in monthly instalments and gave Sybil the chance to acquaint herself with the rest of the plays. By now she was much in demand for local amateur productions as well as those in school, though having been taken by her father to see *The Geisha* and being still nothing if not highly impressionable, her own thoughts had begun to turn toward musical comedy – a theatrical form she did not in fact venture into until around the time of her eightieth birthday. Meanwhile Russell, at school in Windsor, had received a letter from her telling him of her triumph in being accepted as a Guildhall pupil:

We got to the school at ten minutes to eleven, and there was a most glorious noise going on, millions of pianos and violins and singing all going at once ... lots of pupils, about five of them, were sitting on chairs against a wall under a picture of Bach, and one of Wagner opposite, and a girl called Gertrude Meller, older than me, awfully pretty, and a tiny waist, well she was playing some Chopin thing. Oh! Russell, I'll never be able to play like her, she's glorious, she can lift her hand higher than her head, and it always comes down on the right note, and all the time she looks as if it's awfully easy. ... Mother was killing, and went on about me acting and dancing and how I could do them very well and that

I'd danced before Royalty ... so I played a lot then, all without my music – the Beethoven thing you like, more Beethoven things, then a bit of Bach; I felt after the beginning I was getting on finely, then Prof. Berger stopped me and laughed and said, 'Very nice, little girl, very nice', then he turned to Mother and said, 'She has no technique at all; she must give up everything and work at technique.' Mother said, 'Yes, she shall' and I said, 'Oh yes' too; then he said I must give up the violin – oh, I was glad, Russ, and that I must give up games, everything I do with my hands except the piano ... and that I was to practise three hours a day, and then I might possibly be able to play the piano in a few years – I'm so happy I don't know what to do.

So it was weekly trips to the Guildhall, coupled with occasional visits to Her Majesty's where Tree was giving his Mark Antony to the Brutus of Lewis Waller. (Sybil: 'Was I anything like Lewis Waller?', Russell: 'No, not a bit.') Her school reports were still terrible but then again, thought her parents, she was after all to be a pianist and outside the classroom she was not exactly unforthcoming. Had she not, in Russell's view, been the first girl in Rochester to attempt a bicycle ride? Seaside holidays in Devon and Cornwall and Norfolk were the highlights of an otherwise unspectacular teenage life, and when she was sixteen her professor at the Guildhall told Sybil that she was able and ready to start giving piano lessons to younger children. 'Never', said Sybil later, 'had anyone so much to learn and so little to teach'; but to launch the lessons she gave a recital at the Corn Exchange in Rochester on 13 May 1899, taking on Bach, Schumann and Chopin and, according to the ever-present Russell, winning.

Almost immediately afterwards, however, she began to feel pain in her left wrist which rapidly made it almost impossible for her to span an octave; piano cramp was diagnosed and although Sybil persevered for a while at the keyboard, with that dogged tenacity which was already a hallmark of her personality, it was soon clear that she'd be in need of another sort of career: a London specialist told her she'd never manage the practice. Singing, perhaps? Despite a lifetime (thus far at any rate) dedicated almost exclusively 'to the Lord and to the piano', she set off for an audition with the great oratorio teacher Madame Anna Williams. Madame was not impressed ('you have a good ear and a sense of rhythm, but nothing makes a singer but a voice – so I think we'd better say no more') and Sybil went back to the piano, increasingly certain that she'd never be able to make a living at it since her wrist was now inclined to swell up after sustained practice sessions.

As Mother Goose in
parish theatricals,
Rochester, 1895

At the time of her first
piano recital, May
1899

There was of course always the theatre, and Mrs Thorndike, thinking of just that and remembering the school plays, even fixed up an audition for her daughter with Charles Wyndham; on the morning it was due to take place, however, Sybil awoke feeling violently sick and her father decided it was a sign from God warning against a life on the wicked stage.

The next family excitement was a move to Aylesford, also in Kent, where Canon Thorndike was to take up the plum living of the diocese, so known on account of its historic church ('the little cathedral of Kent') and a beautiful vicarage. The happiness and peace of family life there partially made up for the unhappiness Sybil was now going through with her wrist, and parental missions to the needy began to awake in her the romantic though nonetheless devout form of socialism which was, along with her physical endurance, also to be a part of her adult make-up. With the chance of a piano-playing career receding still further, Sybil yet continued with the Guildhall lessons until, one summer afternoon in 1903, when Russell was in the garden at Aylesford, Sybil came home from a day in London:

She burst out 'I'm ready to chuck music as a profession, Russ, and go on the stage with you if you're still keen.' I could see she had been crying or, at any rate, had been feeling pretty bad about it so I tried to restrain my joy and just said, 'Oh it's just the wrist bothering you again. Why not have a rest and then ask Father to let you go abroad and study with someone in Germany for a change?' 'No,' she said. 'I've realised I'm not good enough. If I work and work and work, I'll never be as good as I want to be, and it's not fair to keep on taking fees from Father and Mother, and I ought to earn more ... I can chuck all my pupils – hurrah! – then my temper will improve' ... Sybil was rather violent; we all admitted that, and we always noticed she was in a far nicer frame of mind when she was acting ... we got a newspaper and read advertisements of Schools of Acting till we came to 'Ben Greet's Academy'. 'Well, we know he's a darling, don't we?' said Sybil, 'because we followed him home once, about a year ago, from Chatham Theatre ... and he looked sweet. And he's awfully keen on church – we've found that out too.'

Philip Ben Greet (the knighthood wasn't to come until 1929) had founded his acting school just off the Strand in 1896 but at the time Sybil and Russell applied he was in fact touring America and, as Sybil later recalled for Elizabeth Sprigge, it was Greet's colleague Frederick Topham who held the audition:

So I went up with Mother. Oh, I looked such a sight! I put on a veil, God knows why! We climbed up the stairs – it was in Bedford Street in an awful room high up on about the fourth floor. And there was that little man, Fred Topham, a wonderful principal and a brilliant old actor. 'Well, would the girl like to do something for me?' he said, and then he gazed at me and added, 'No, I don't think I'll bother her to do anything – she looks as if she can act.' And I said, 'Of course I can act, I've acted since I was four. Anybody can act, it's the easiest thing in the world.'

Although the Thorndike parents had been fully expecting Russell to go to Cambridge and then into the church, while Sybil made her career as a concert pianist, they settled with surprising equanimity if not actual resignation for the fact that both children were now to be pupils of Greet's: 'Their lives', said Mrs Thorndike later, 'were theirs to lead and our part was to act merely as guides'. So Sybil and Russell enrolled at the Academy the following autumn, and after half a term Topham gave their mother his verdict: 'The girl has great gifts, I think, especially in character and comedy. I see no tragic quality. The boy is harder to judge. He's odd and unexpected; I think he should be a clown.'

Sybil was not pleased ('I can play tragedy better than anybody – just give me the chance'), but by the summer Greet himself had returned from America and the school was told he'd be in front at their end-of-term performance of Pinero's *The Cabinet Minister*. Sybil at twenty-one ('and terribly raw for my age') was cast as the forty-year-old Lady Twombley and prepared for it by walking around with books on her head to improve her deportment. After the matinée, B.G. (as Greet was forever known) told their parents that he'd like Sybil to join him for his next American tour in the late summer, and Russell to stay with one of his English touring companies until the following year when he too could cross the Atlantic with the Greet players.

It was agreed, then, that Sybil should sail with the company on 24 August 1904. There being a month or two in hand, she joined up with Greet's Pastoral Players and made her professional début as an actress playing Palmis in *The Palace of Truth* with Matheson Lang in the grounds of Downing College, Cambridge, on 14 June; later she also walked on for Greet in productions of *The Merry Wives of Windsor* and *My Lord from Town*, the latter also staged in Oxford and Cambridge college gardens by the Greet players. During *The Palace of Truth*, reports Russell, a tremendous backstage row erupted between Sybil and the Cambridge stage manager who had reprimanded her for talking through other actors' laughs and giving the audience no chance to react to her own short scene:

# Worcester College Gardens,

## OXFORD,

*(By kind permission of the Rev. the Provost and Fellows).*

### FRIDAY, JUNE 17, 1904,

At 8.30 o'clock    -    'THE PALACE OF TRUTH.'

### SATURDAY, JUNE 18,

At 2.30 o'clock   -   -   'MY LORD FROM TOWN.'

At 8.30 o'clock 'THE MERRY WIVES OF WINDSOR.'

# MR. BEN GREET'S

## WELL-KNOWN COMPANY OF

# → PASTORAL ᛭ PLAYERS. ←

This is the Twentieth Season under MR. GREET'S Management of these

# → Open=Air Plays, ←

*And the Public and Press have been unanimous in their praise.*

| | | |
|---|---|---|
| General Manager .. .. | } For MR. BEN GREET { | Mr. FREDERIC TOPHAM |
| Stage Manager .. .. .. | | Mr. CYRIL CATTLEY |
| Master of the Greensward .. | | Mr. F. DARCH |

PRICES:—RESERVED AND NUMBERED SEATS, **5/-**.   UNRESERVED SEATS, **3/-**.
PROMENADE, **2/-**.

A BOARDED FLOOR WILL BE LAID ON THE GRASS.

*Tickets can be obtained at the New Theatre Box Office, from 11 to 4, and at the Garden Gate an hour before each Performance.*

Entrance by the Garden Gate in Worcester Street at 7.30, and Matinee at 1.30 o'clock, when a Selection of Music, under the Conductorship of Mr. LONG, will be performed.

BEAUTIFUL LIME-LIGHT EFFECTS.     THE GARDENS WILL BE ILLUMINATED.

*In the event of wet weather the Performances will take place in the New Theatre.*

VINCENT, PRINTER, OXFORD.

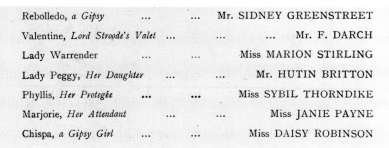

| | |
|---|---|
| Rebolledo, *a Gipsy* ... ... | Mr. SIDNEY GREENSTREET |
| Valentine, *Lord Stroode's Valet* ... ... ... | Mr. F. DARCH |
| Lady Warrender ... ... | Miss MARION STIRLING |
| Lady Peggy, *Her Daughter* ... ... | Mr. HUTIN BRITTON |
| Phyllis, *Her Protegée* ... ... | Miss SYBIL THORNDIKE |
| Marjorie, *Her Attendant* ... ... | Miss JANIE PAYNE |
| Chispa, *a Gipsy Girl* ... ... | Miss DAISY ROBINSON |

The Oxford programme for the Ben Greet Company in the week of her professional stage début, June 1904

'I can't stand audiences' [Sybil told me]. 'Just as I'm thoroughly enjoying myself they must go and interrupt and laugh or something – it's too sickening.' I told her gently that the audience was the most important part of the theatre, and that we and all other good actors were the servants of that audience. 'I'm not,' she said, 'I do it because I want to do it and to earn my living. I don't care a bit for any of the faces sitting in front ... their bit of money doesn't pay for what we give them. If they give as much as we give – all of themselves – then they'll get back something worth having ... you don't get anything by just paying money for it; you've got to do something yourself.'

The worker-audience philosophy was one that was to stay with Sybil until her dying day; actor and spectator were, in her view, equally obliged to labour in order to bring a performance into action, and although never slow to take the blame for her own disasters when she felt that blame rightfully hers, Sybil (like Lilian Baylis) was not slow either to point out when an audience failed for some reason to attain the high standards of attentiveness and enthusiasm which she always expected of it.

# Greet's Girl

Sybil was in America for more than a year on that first Greet tour, and every day she wrote home to the family – long, gossipy, evocative letters treasured by Russell and many others sent direct to the Canon and rediscovered, neatly stored, after his death. The first was posted just before her ship sailed from Greenock in August 1904:

It's a lovely morning; the ship doesn't look very large, I suppose she's all right ... but we've just had the best breakfast I can remember. B.G. paid for [his niece] Daisy and me, 'for luck' he said – wasn't it decent of him? Heavenly bloaters with soft roes, tons of toast and tea and marmalade. B.G. said, 'Is this your usual appetite? Because you'll have to be careful not to get fat.' I said, 'I'm always hungry in the morning and near the water.' We've just come on board and seen our cabins. I'm not with anyone I know, and there isn't a porthole – it's what they call an inside cabin – but there are three American ladies with me; they seem awfully nice, though how we are ever going to get dressed in the small space I can't think. I don't suppose any of us will ever wash during the whole voyage – it's about three miles to the bathroom and I loathe washing in bits, don't you?

Company talk on the voyage ranged over the current state of the English theatre in general and of Bernard Shaw's writing in particular, but Sybil (although she'd done an amateur *You Never Can Tell* the previous May) showed little interest, being understandably more absorbed with the Atlantic:

I've loved every minute of it except the seasick bit. Ben Greet told me the other day that it was going to be very hard work, and was I a quick study? I said, 'Yes, awfully quick,' and he said, 'Well, you'd better learn everybody's parts, because you never know when you may have to go on.' So I'm starting on *Hamlet* because I know all *Twelfth Night* and a good bit of *As You Like It*. I learn parts first thing after breakfast, when I've had a good walk around the deck. ... I rather spoilt my new Shakespeare yesterday. It was awfully rough and I was sitting next to a French lady who was eating semolina pudding – we'd had lunch on deck. Suddenly an enormous wave broke the rope by which our chairs were tied, and we all slid to the lee-scuppers – at least I think they are the lee-scuppers – and my Shakespeare and the semolina pudding got all mixed up in them. The French lady shouted out *Nous allons* and so we did. It's rather sickening, as Margy Smith gave me the Shakespeare and it's a beauty. Semolina pudding and salt water have made it look perfectly awful. We always call the French lady *Nous allons* now – she is great fun.

That tone of breathless schoolgirl enthusiasm, faintly surprising perhaps in a writer about to be twenty-two, may have been the result of a comparatively sheltered Victorian upbringing in Rochester; more plausibly, it may have been consciously used by Sybil to mask the fact that the ship (*The Numidian*) was as she admitted later 'truly terrible' and about to be condemned. Soon however there was the Statue of Liberty to rejoice at:

You feel that every nation can come to America and earn their livings and have adventures and not worry any more. It's wonderful to see a land that opens its doors to every one isn't it? I suppose England does that too, only when one is in a country one doesn't realise it quite the same. We took ages going through the Customs. I simply adored the man who turned my trunks upside down – he had the killingest voice – dreadful – and he clicked his teeth like that awful girl at the Brighton Cricket Week, and he said, 'Got any nooooo clothes?' and I said, 'Every single thing in my trunk is new. I wouldn't risk having to buy anything here because I've heard it's so expensive.'

The next few weeks were spent, Sybil later recalled, 'travelling thousands and thousands of miles to big towns and one-eyed towns all over the country from coast to coast ... coining adjectives in trying to describe to myself and the family at home the wonders of this land seen through my very young, Walt Whitman-dazzled eyes and brains and feeling'. There was a pastoral performance on Long Island with Sybil playing Phoebe in *As You Like It* ('B.G. cut some of her long speech ... I felt rather sick about that until I discovered he was cutting everyone's part.'), and then a brisk look at Niagara:

It seemed as if I'd no business to be the only one in my family seeing such a sight. You know what it looks like in pictures – well, that's nothing to it – it's only the tiniest idea of what it's like, and the more you look, and the more you think about it, the more extraordinary you feel. I'm sure it's far better for people than church, because you don't *believe* in God – you *know* it, Niagara makes you know it.... PS Later, had an enormous meal. Thoroughly enjoyed it. Two helps of everything and hoped B.G. wouldn't notice. As B.G.

walked out of the dining car he said, 'Old fat Syb'. It made me feel rather depressed.

The letters give slight hints of an attachment to Eric Blind who was playing Orsino in *Twelfth Night* ('he's got the most lovely face I've ever seen in my life, don't you think so too?') but apart from that and one disastrous matinée when under his breath Greet whispered across the stage to her that she looked more like a ragbag than Olivia's gentlewoman, the tour passed quietly enough and there was even time between rehearsals and whistle stops to discuss with one of the leading ladies, Mrs Love aptly enough, Sybil's forced renunciation of the piano for the theatre:

Somehow or other Mrs Love drew it all out of me, how I felt about shirking music and living only happily, and she was very wise about it all. She said that the acting art was different because you don't employ an artificial medium (sounds good that, doesn't it?). She means that you don't have to learn a new language like notes and strings, but she says that if I look at it properly it's just as hard – that the medium I use is myself, and I must make myself as perfect as I want ... not only walking and dancing, moving and speaking beautifully, but mind, too. ...

In Chicago, Greet took them to see E. H. Sothern and Julia Marlowe in *Romeo and Juliet*:

Fancy seeing Niagara and *Romeo and Juliet* for the first time in one week! I've never heard anything more glorious than Julia Marlowe ... she is rather square and not very thin but she'd not been going long before I'd forgotten all this and I saw only the young lovely Italian girl. I can't tell you what I felt during the Balcony Scene. You know how love bores me – well, it wouldn't if it was like *Romeo and Juliet*. ... I thought I never would stop crying. Oh! I'd love to play Juliet ... but I don't suppose anyone would want me to, I don't look tragic-romantic, do I? How I wish I did. ...

Ten years later, at the Baylis Vic, she was to play Portia, Rosalind, Constance, Beatrice, Imogen and Ophelia; but Juliet, in the course of a long and crowded Shakespearian career, never.

By the time they reached California Sybil was getting twenty-five dollars a week and living frugally enough (often sharing a bed with Greet's niece Daisy, still her best friend on the tour) to save most of it. She had however developed an unfortunate tendency to giggle on stage, especially during Greet's long soliloquy in the *Hamlet* court scene; Greet was predictably not amused, and fined her two dollars for misbehaving. And then, in San Francisco, Sybil and her beloved girlfriend Dai were taken to a funfair by an over-amorous journalist:

A dreadful little man: he's a Jew, but I always like Jews so tremendously. This isn't one of the best sort ... finally he said to me, 'You ought to have been a boy, you haven't got the instincts of a girl,' and I said, 'No I haven't. I wish I was a boy, and tonight I wish I was a boy more than ever.' Dai said I looked so huffy she nearly died, so then we all went on a sort of mild switchback in a boat, and there were tunnels, and he would hold my hand, and I gave myself up for lost. What misery it is being a girl – how I loathe men who get keen on me – oh dear me, I feel so relieved to think I won't ever marry, I couldn't stand anyone saying 'in love' things to me all the time. I shall adopt lots of children, and you and I will live together, Russ, won't we? Much more fun than lots of hateful people married to you. ...

The journalist got his own back by telling Greet that Sybil had legs like a grand piano, but then he was forgotten and it was on to 'all sorts of lovely places called San José and Monterey and heaps of other places beginning with San and Santa'. Then, in Stockton, California, came the big chance:

I played Viola last night! Mrs Crawley didn't feel at all well on the train and Mr Crawley came to me (Oh! he's a perfect lamb with the nicest face, rather like Cassius) and he said, 'Do you know Viola?' and I said, 'Rather, I should say I did' ... so I relieved his mind of all doubts as to my ability and then I prayed hard – and oh! Father what I wanted to pray was this: 'Oh Lord God, please smite her with a fell disease so that she can't play for weeks, and let me play the parts, oh! Lord.' But no, not your good, Christian, kind little daughter. I said meekly, 'Oh Lord God, please make her better, but let it be necessary for her to have one night off at least.' And the Lord hearkened unto my prayer for as soon as I'd unpacked my bag at Stockton (praying all the while, you may be quite sure) a message was sent from B.G. to say would I run thro' the words with some of the company in the afternoon. ... I felt too terribly thrilled to eat much, and Dai was too sweet the way she helped me to dress and kept on saying things like 'For goodness sake, Syb, keep your knees straight' and 'don't waggle your head at every word when you get emotional and you'll be all right' ... Well I've never enjoyed myself so much in all my life. In fact I felt I *was* Viola, she didn't seem different to anything I felt deep down – and when Sebastian comes in the end and I saw him, I felt exactly like seeing you, Russ, after years and ages of separation and I cried like anything but it didn't matter really, did it? The audience were lovely and laughed at everything I wanted them to laugh at, which was most kind. Ben Greet said, 'Good girl, you never missed a word,' and Dai said, 'It was lovely, Syb, and you only waggled your head once badly, and I never even looked at your knees because I was enjoying it all so' ... the paper (they have a special one even in a tiny place like this – the Americans do seem to care so much about papers) said, 'Mrs Crawley' (they didn't know it wasn't her, you see) 'gave a most charming performance, naïve and touching.' Ha! ha! now my foot is on the ladder truly and really, and I mean to swot terribly hard to know every single part, in case any kind person gets stricken with the plague and can't appear.

From there to Vancouver for Christmas, where she found Sidney Greenstreet in church ('enormous and such a dear'), and south again through California and on to Salt Lake City, Denver and Kansas City, where the obliging Mrs Crawley fell headlong down a staircase, thereby allowing Sybil to play for her in *Everyman* as well as taking over Beatrice in *Much Ado* and Rosalind in *As You Like It*. Greet then started another of his 'pastoral' tours and the company played an open-air *Tempest*, ruined, according to the local paper, 'by the unseemly levity of one of the goddesses, Miss Sybil Thorndike'. She'd accidentally fallen over and then succumbed to one of her by now well-known giggling fits, to the fury of Greet who fined her another two dollars and told her not to be so fat and foolish in future.

By the end of August, a year and a month after she'd first set sail from Greenock, Sybil was back at Tilbury being met by her mother who, as appalled as Greet by her chubbiness, said she now looked 'just like a little German girl', and would be unlikely to get any more work on the stage until she thinned down again. Sybil promised to do so, adding that in any case she'd be setting off for a second American tour in a month's time, her money now raised to thirty-five dollars a week and with the promise that Russell could go with them.

# 1905-1912

# The Casson Man

The second American tour continued much as the first, with a mixture of open-air pastorals and indoor performances of the Bard; Sybil reckoned by the end of it that she'd played (in all but four of the United States) 112 separate parts ranging from Everyman to Viola and often three or four smaller ones played within a single evening. Rampaging through the cast lists, depending on who was ill, absent or otherwise engaged, Sybil collected some remarkable experience and was often lucky enough to cut her theatre teeth so far away from expert gaze (other than that of Greet himself who was increasingly avuncular towards her) that she might as well have been playing on the moon. Many of the company believed that the illness-rate among those whom Sybil was understudying had become altogether too high for comfort, but the training she got (playing night after night either in halls or the open air, hardly ever a conventional theatre) was to stand her in good stead for Chichester half a century later. She also made a remarkable number of friends along the way including Woodrow Wilson, then a professor at Princeton, whom she and Russell had met on the boat going back to America in 1905. Some months later, and still on the tour, there was an accident which very nearly ended Sybil's career as an actress; she herself told the story to Michael MacOwan:

I was playing at Princeton University and Russell and I were staying with Woodrow Wilson who was then President of the University. We were playing on the campus – I was playing Good Deeds in *Everyman* – and I opened my mouth and drew in my breath, and a piece of powder-puff which was on my veil flew into my throat and got stuck round my vocal cords and I couldn't speak. I did a lot of acting, but I couldn't say another word! And that began my struggle with voice. I worked for nearly three months in the open air with a false (forced) voice. Of course I ought to have been silent then for at least a week. I went to a doctor the next day, who said my vocal cords were clear, but they were a little swollen. And then I went on working until finally it got so bad that Russell said, 'Sybil's got to go home. She must see a doctor.' I came home and I saw a top specialist, Sir St Clair Thompson who was King Edward's throat doctor. And he looked at my throat and said, 'Are you a brave girl?' And I said, 'Yes I am.' And he said, 'I'm afraid you won't speak on the stage again.' Wasn't that awful! And he said, 'Your vocal cords are smothered with growths. I can't see anything. I can't see a vocal cord at all. But if you could possibly be silent for six weeks, I might see if it is curable. So go out of this room, don't speak another word for six weeks. Have a notebook, and write everything down; and when you come back, into my room, in six weeks' time, I can tell you if it's curable.' Not a word did I speak – I practised the piano, I went for long walks in the country. I was staying at the vicarage, of course, with my father and mother. And then, when I went back to the specialist in six weeks, he looked at my throat, and I was sitting in perfect terror. He said, 'You've got the constitution of an ox, those growths have all gone, your vocal cords are clear. Now,' he said, 'you've got to be jolly careful.' Then I went to a person and worked. He was quite a quack, but he knew how to get me over the first difficulties and so I got my voice back again.

Russell (who wielded a greater influence over his sister's life and career than anyone until the meeting with Lewis Casson in 1908) had by now returned to join Greet's company in America, and Sybil was left alone in London to pick up the threads of her career as best she could. But the joy of getting her natural voice back (she'd expected at best a deep growl) encouraged her to audition for Tree, who turned her down, and then for Nigel Playfair, who got her a Sunday-night job with the Play Actors' Society, first as O Chicka San in *His Japanese Wife* and then as an American girl in a farce called *The Marquis* by Cecil Raleigh.

By one of those accidental miracles of which theatrical biographies are largely comprised, Bernard Shaw was in front and next morning Sybil had a note from Playfair: 'Shaw saw your ridiculous play last night – liked you very much – says you might do as the understudy for Ellen O'Malley in *Candida*. Come along quick and read the part.'

*Candida*, written during 1894 and 1895, had already been seen several times in London, first in a Stage Society production at the Royal Strand and then for several performances in Vedrenne–Barker seasons at the Royal Court, but the present tour was going out under the partial aegis of Miss Horniman, a lady as legendary and as important as Miss Baylis in the creation of an English repertory system. Shaw however was at that time less than wildly enthusiastic about her Manchester company and insisted that, if they were to play his *Candida*, Playfair should form a subsidiary company. For that, Sybil auditioned:

I read it and, my dear, I put everything I'd got into it – Lady Macbeth, Everyman, Beatrice, everything; and when I'd finished with a bounce, Shaw rocked with laughing. He said, 'Splendid, my dear young lady, you go home and have a husband and children and do the housekeeping and (then) you'll be a very good Candida; but you'll do for the understudy.' And he said, 'You're understudying one of the most beautiful actresses I know, Ellen O'Malley' and that was a great joy – Shaw loved her very much. And at rehearsals Shaw had me sitting next to him, at the table, and explaining (with his wonderful manners) everything as it went along. And do you know, he did say a lovely thing to me – mustn't sound conceited – but he did say, 'You've got something that Janet Achurch had.' He said, 'Work, you work, watch everything and you'll do it' ... he could only be virulent when he'd got his pen in his hand, and on the platform in debate ... but I don't think he could say an unkind thing to people, he was so full of feeling for them ... before *Candida* we had a front piece because *Candida* wasn't considered a full evening's length in those days. It was a rather racy play by Havelock Ellis, you know, the sex man, and I played the leading part in it. We started off the tour under the aegis of Miss Horniman at Belfast. Miss Horniman's Manchester company was playing the first three days of the week, and we played the last three days. I went in front, on the first night, and I saw a young man playing Trench in *Widowers' Houses*.

The 'young man' was Lewis Casson. Then thirty-two and therefore seven years older than Sybil almost to the day, he'd been brought up in North Wales where his father managed a bank and later designed organs; the same strains of music and devout churchgoing ran through his family background as they did through that of the Thorndikes, and, like Russell, Lewis had been originally destined for the church. To pay for a theological training, he became a schoolmaster in London but then got caught up in the amateur theatre; in 1903 he'd turned professional, and then spent the greater part of the next three years in the Shaw seasons at the Court playing in everything from *Man and Superman* to *Captain Brassbound's Conversion*. By 1908 he'd also worked with Poel and with Oscar Asche, but Shaw and the Vedrenne–Barker management had exerted the greatest influence on him and he was now one of a gradually widening group of young and politically committed actors determined not only to set up away from London an alternative to the high-society theatre of the old West End actor-managers, but also to bring the theatre into the arena of debate over such issues as women's suffrage and the 'new socialism'.

In sharp contrast, Sybil was still very much 'the vicar's daughter', an image of innocence, naïvety and a kind of gauche unworldliness which

was to cling to her for several years to come. Still, she did like the look
of Casson:

At that time I was very devoted to a certain cousin of mine, really rather in
love with him [Basil Bowers] and I thought Lewis looked like Basil. . . . I loved
the very incisive way he spoke. And then I went round afterwards and was introduced to him but he never spoke a word to me; he was changing his shoes,
very quick and you know the way he talks – very sharp. Then the next day, out
in the street, I met him again, and again he never spoke a word to me but talked
to May Playfair; so then nothing happened. We went off to Dublin for the next
week, and May Playfair and I went off to the zoo; and there, in the lion house,
was Lewis Casson, trying to make the lioness go to sleep by mesmerising her.
And I thought that was a nice thing to do. So we walked all round the place
together, but he never spoke a word to me, he talked to May Playfair – they
talked shop the whole time. Then we sat down to have a cup of tea and afterwards
I said, 'Well I'm going into the lion house again, because there's one lion I want
to have a look at.' And Lewis said, 'I'll come too.' So he came, and we stood
in front of the cages and I thought, 'I wish I were a boy. That's the sort of man
I'd like to have for a pal' . . . and that began it.

'It' took a little time, Sybil's sexual innocence being such that she'd
managed to travel all through America twice without ever learning the
facts of life; she was however now rising twenty-six and her letters to
Russell suggest that by the summer of 1908 she at last knew what was
happening to her:

The highbrows [in the company] follow Shaw and Granville Barker, and
people like John Galsworthy and Arnold Bennett are all highbrows, and people
talk of them in an odd and very familiar voice and you feel when you listen
to them that you are very cheap and that if you aren't careful you'll drop your
aitches or giggle, but I keep a tight hold on myself. There's a boy called Basil
Dean with a very special highbrow face, and one called Clarence Derwent who
is a wit and makes jokes that I'm beginning to see; but they're too clever.
They're all interested in politics, and the prince of this lot is this man Casson. . . .
Nigel says his clothes are appalling . . . but then I can never see what's wrong
with my own clothes and every one says I look like the devil in real life . . . he
wears a very shabby overcoat and a hat all down over his eyes like a tramp –
looks as if he would fight you if you gave him a chance . . . but he's got a really
lovely voice.

Having spent so much of her early career in America, Sybil had in fact
totally missed all the Vedrenne–Barker work at the Court and with it
the start of what she now called 'highbrow' acting; she'd also missed the

Greet's girl as Ceres in *The Tempest*, America, 1904–1907

Miss Horniman's Company, The Gaiety, Manchester, 1908. Miss Horniman herself (*inset*), Lewis Casson (*far left, back row*), Basil Dean (*sixth from left, back row*), Sybil Thorndike (*second from left, seated*), and Ben Iden Payne (*fourth from left, seated*)

start of Miss Horniman's pioneering repertory work in London, Dublin and Manchester, but within a few weeks of her return voiceless to England here she was working in Shaw for Miss Horniman with the best of them. And her instinctive love for Casson rapidly soothed her ruffled dislike of the 'highbrows' like Lewis:

He's raving mad about the theatre, and he looks as if he ought to be an engineer or a sailor or something to do with real life – not a bit like an actor, but fearfully highbrow; at least, I'm changing about highbrows – when it's affected it's highbrow but when it's real it's enormously interesting and it's a new way of looking at acting that these people have. I mean, they're not in the least exciting like you and me, Russ, you can't imagine them making such terrible faces that they'd frighten people like you and I can, but they're being very real and very restrained and nothing actory in their acting. It's rather attractive. I'm starting to try it; you probably won't recognize me when you come home.

After Dublin the two companies divided, and Sybil's *Candida* group continued to tour: Basil Dean remembers himself and them later that year in Brighton:

Sybil brought to the company her own special quality of enthusiasm and a personality better suited to the serenity of the cathedral close than the stridency of Grand Guignol or the thunder of Greek tragedy. Her Candida was the finest I ever saw. We spent a joyful fortnight, swimming off the pier every morning and scandalising holiday audiences with Shaw's *Widowers' Houses* at night. Sybil joined our swimming party with glee; but neither we nor the lonely stunt man who dived off the pier head twice daily on a bicycle was the centre of attraction for the onlookers; that was Marie Lloyd, plopping intrepidly into the deep sea in a billowing costume to a chorus of laughter and chaff from her music-hall companions.

For Sybil, the tour meant regular work and then a longer engagement at the Gaiety Manchester where Iden Payne was now in charge. Sybil was to understudy, and occasionally play, most of the major female leads:

I had to learn these parts very quickly and Lewis Casson being a very kind man said, 'Would you like me to help you get these parts into your head? I'm rather good at doing that.' I said, 'Oh if only you would.' And we went up onto the roof of the theatre and then we became great friends and did walks together and well, there we are and that was it.

But in her letters to Russell, there were still only occasional indications of how things were shaping up:

The Casson man and I walked together and I made him talk to me about himself. He's had rather the same upbringing as us – you know, all holy and church and being able to laugh at it because you know it too well to be solemn, which is gladdening to my heart. I'm not falling in love, so don't worry – he's much too nice; and he told me that he wasn't going to marry until he could afford a valet and a secretary because he couldn't be bothered, and I said, 'I'm just like you, I have never intended to marry. Russell and I are always going to live with each other' so that's all right . . . you'll be home in the summer, won't you, angel? I've got such yards to tell you about this new acting – very different to Shakespeare but I think Shakespeare would be all the better for a dose of it. . . . Casson's acting interests me – you're frightfully conscious of a brain, not so much that he's become the person but as if he was making you see the person and he was giving you suggestions – it's not the way I work, but it's very interesting and his speed is most exhilarating. I do detest people who, if they're saying something either beautiful or important, go three times slower in case you miss anything. By the time some of them have got to the end of a sentence, you've forgotten the beginning and then you're lost. Casson speaks nearly as fast as you think.

But it wasn't only in the theatre that Lewis Casson was becoming Sybil's guide and mentor, as she explained in another of her many letters to Russell:

There's another thing – and that's politics. Manchester is full of politics and there's a war on between Winston Churchill and Joynson Hicks – it's the election. Do you know anything at all about politics? I don't, except that you're supposed to vote Conservative if you're respectable and be anything but a socialist. Well, most of these highbrows are socialists – full of 'the people'. Lloyd George, who is a Liberal, was down here yesterday and Casson took me to the meeting. Oh, he's Welsh, Lloyd George, and so is Lewis Casson, but I gather the Welsh are a rather slippery race the way Welshmen talk. I did enjoy myself at this meeting. I don't think I'm going to be Conservative any more – it's so boring.

Well, and there's Women Suffrage [sic] too. You know, Russ, I'm terribly ignorant. I said to Lewis Casson, 'Whatever do you want to go fussing like this – there's only just enough time to learn about acting without wanting votes and such-like.' He said, 'Your acting won't be much good if you don't think about the world in which we live and the conditions of the people.' I said, 'But I don't want to think all the time about the world – there are much more exciting worlds that help me much more with acting. You all go on as if this mattered more than *Alice in Wonderland*.' He never answered, only smiled (but not an understanding smile; thank God he never 'understands', he only wants to fight – so pleasant) then said, 'Well, the sooner you learn about Women's Suffrage the better. I'll take you to a meeting tomorrow after rehearsal.'

Within a week, such was the force of Lewis's guidance and the strength of her own glowing enthusiasm for anything new, Sybil was chairing a meeting of Manchester suffragettes – and within ten days she'd met Mrs Pankhurst:

Off I trundled with Lewis to the Free Trade Hall where Mrs Pankhurst and daughter Christabel were speaking. I was entranced, first thinking what a lovely part Mrs Pankhurst would be to play. But, you know, she got me right from the start – quietly dramatic, dignified, and such well-chosen phrases. I thought well, she'd convert anyone. Then up got Christabel: more violent, with wild arm movements, too much I thought, but exciting. Well, from then on with much instruction from Lewis, I began to think about Votes for Women.

Another tour followed, with Sybil playing Candida under Lewis's guidance at Exeter; then they went to Birmingham, from where Russell received the letter he'd been expecting for quite some time:

Lewis Casson has asked me to marry him. I'm so taken aback. He's never even called me by my christian name. I didn't fall flat on my face when he proposed in the Kardomah Restaurant over coffee and toast, but the whole room spun round and so did the houses outside. So I suppose it means I shall marry him, though everything doesn't look quite as Mother says it ought to when you're in love. I really don't feel as if he's on earth at all, so I expect it comes to the same thing.

The family at Aylesford were appalled. Mrs Thorndike felt that Casson was in no position to give Sybil the elegant life she deserved, and the Canon travelled straight to Carlisle (where the company now was) to discourage his daughter. Casson refused to meet him at first, but hid behind the milk churns on Carlisle station to catch a glimpse of his prospective father-in-law getting off the train. Later however they did get together in Sybil's lodgings and the following week at Blackpool they were joined by Mrs Thorndike who, after the predictable row about the kind of wedding they should have, also settled for the situation.

Later that autumn, in the refurbished Manchester Gaiety, Lewis and Sybil played together in the first show to be written and directed by Basil Dean; called *Marriages are Made in Heaven*, it won them all good notices from James Agate in the *Manchester Guardian*. 'I arrived at the theatre for the first rehearsal,' recalled Dean, 'with my heart thumping like a rickety gas engine, to find the actors having a brisk argument among themselves in a corner. But when Sybil saw me she immediately turned to the others with that all-embracing gesture of hers, and said "Now come along, don't be silly. Let's all help the young man to have a success".'

The marriage was fixed for Christmas 1908 and just before it the company were again on tour, playing *Candida* in Ireland with Sybil again in the title role and Lewis now no longer making notes on her performance from the wings but playing opposite her as Marchbanks. Sybil later recalled the events of the next few days for Elizabeth Sprigge:

Lewis and I were to be married at Aylesford the following Tuesday and we simply had to catch our train back to Dublin (on the Saturday night) so as not to miss the boat. We reduced *Candida* to something like an hour, by sheer speed. People who came in a little late found we were in the middle of the second act. We went straight down to Aylesford and on Monday there was a big to-do in the barn, Lewis making a fatuous speech about taking away 'the jewel of the village' . . . on the morning of the wedding, Lewis and I went to Early Service together and as we came out I remember him saying, 'I feel awful about taking you away from all this.' And I was crying. I felt 'I can't bear leaving Aylesford. I can't bear to leave home' . . . Father gave me away, wearing his cassock, and I had two Bishops to marry me – the Bishop of Rochester and my uncle the Bishop of Thetford.

On a month's leave granted by Miss Horniman, the newly-wed Cassons spent their honeymoon visiting his family in Wales and on a fourteen-day walking tour of Derbyshire. Then it was back to the Gaiety for a revival of Galsworthy's *The Silver Box* which Lewis had played in during the first London run three years earlier. Then came a full rep. schedule of weekly changeovers together with the occasional North of England tour before, in June, the Horniman company travelled south for a brief but successful London season at the Coronet Theatre. Titles like *When the Devil was Ill, The Feud, Trespassers will be Prosecuted* and *The Vale of Content* give a fair indication of the range of Sybil's stage work at this time, though she did also do Lady Denison in Hankin's *The Charity that Began at Home*, acting, said C. E. Montague, 'with faultless intelligence and humour'. But after the season in Notting Hill Gate, Lewis took her, on a motorcycle, back to Aylesford to await the birth of their first child, due in October. He, John Casson, was not however to be born in Kent because in the later summer Canon Thorndike was offered the living of St James the Less in Westminster and the family moved there. A neighbour, also a man of the church married to an Agnes, was to be Father Gerard Olivier whose son, Laurence, Sybil first saw acting in school plays nearby.

Soon after John's birth Sybil went back to work and by March 1910 she and Lewis had both got jobs with the Granville Barker–Charles Froh-man repertory company (the first of many attempts at a National Theatre) at the Duke of York's, on the strength of which they rented a flat next door to the Thorndike's new vicarage. Not that the money was all that good: Frohman had a starry company with Boucicault and Granville Barker as directors and Irene Vanbrugh, Lillah McCarthy and Hilda Trevelyan as the leading ladies, so that the most that was available for Sybil was three pounds ten shillings a week (thirty shillings less than she'd been getting in Manchester) and seven pounds for Lewis. Still, it was a chance not to be missed. The season ran six months and in Russell's view was what really established both Sybil and Lewis in the eyes and memories of London audiences. There were small parts for her in Meredith's *The Sentimentalists* and Granville Barker's *The Madras House* but then, late in the season, came a play by Elizabeth Baker called *Chains*, a 'suburban tragedy' which Lillah McCarthy didn't want to do and in which the leading role therefore fell to Sybil.

Boucicault directed her sharply, restraining her old urge to act in capital letters ('Not one single thing I do is right for him', Sybil complained after rehearsal one day. 'My face moves too much, my body moves too much, I do everything too much. Mr Boucicault says if I stop doing everything and do nothing at all he thinks I shall be a great success in the part.') and the outcome was a triumph. Frohman himself came over from New York, saw Sybil in *Chains* and immediately offered both Cassons an American season.

John was only nine months old, and Sybil was understandably nervous about leaving him; but her mother agreed to take him into the vicarage with her and a nurse, and although there was no money in the bank there was the promise of American riches to come. So they borrowed twenty pounds from an actors' fund and set off for New York – Lewis's first American visit and Sybil's third in ten years. The play for which Frohman wanted them both was Somerset Maugham's *Smith* with Mary Boland and John Drew (the Barrymores' uncle) in the leading roles. 'Cynicism driven to its highest pitch', said J. T. Grein of the original London production in the previous year, but in New York it did well enough and Sybil did so well that Frohman offered her a national tour together with the guarantee of three months in New York every year in a different play.

The offer was obviously too good to refuse, even though both Cassons disliked it on two scores: it would keep them away from England and their new baby; and it meant doing the same show over and over again from town to town at a time when they had both become totally hooked on the repertory system of six or even eight different plays a week. Eventually, and admittedly in order to get out of the Frohman contract, they started another baby. Then, while they were playing in Salt Lake City, came the news that Iden Payne was leaving the Gaiety Manchester and that Miss Horniman would like Lewis to take it over. Explaining their respective maternal and professional situations to a courteous and understanding Frohman, they abandoned America once Lewis had seen California and were home in time for the birth of Christopher Casson in January 1912.

# To the Vic

Back in Manchester and now in charge, Lewis opened with a *Twelfth Night* which, said the local *Courier*, 'for pure mirthfulness and artistry has never been surpassed'; he then took his entire company off on a Canadian tour, doing nearly a dozen plays over six weeks and leaving Sybil in a house near Heaton Park to cope with her two young sons. A cook-general was soon engaged, however, and by June Sybil was in London to create Beatrice in *Hindle Wakes*, Stanley Houghton's drama (one that Sybil subsequently filmed) made famous by its classic 'Should Fanny marry Alan?' poster. A friend of the Cassons at this time, and a regular Gaiety theatre-goer, was the dramatist Eden Phillpotts, who recalled:

One memory clings to my mind from Manchester: the wondrous versatility of Sybil Thorndike. Even as a girl, for she was little more at that time, I marked her rare sense of humour in a comic part she was just then playing at night, and watched her rehearsing by day a stricken heroine with every apt and poignant emotion, mien and gesture, even to the expression on her face and the woe in her voice. Comedy and tragedy are alike to her and always were, for she has that protean gift to lose herself in any character, having grasped its intrinsic nature.

The Frohman savings and Horniman salaries took care of any immediate financial worries, and between June 1912 and May 1913 both Sybil and Lewis were happily employed at the Gaiety, he concentrating more and more on the directing work which would from now on be his chief interest and she already (as was her later wont) reviving earlier successes like *The Charity that Began at Home* and adding to them new work such as the Barker–Housman *Prunella* and, most notably, St John Ervine's *Jane Clegg*. Her success in the title role (an anglicized Ibsenite Nora expelling an errant husband) led to a London summer season at the Court; then it was back to the Gaiety, where Lewis had devised a repertory exchange system with Basil Dean's company at Liverpool so that each city could show its best theatrical productions to the other – one of a number of regional-rep. innovations for which the English theatre still has to thank his pioneering efforts.

Late in 1913 however came a parting of the ways: Lewis had decided to stage *Julius Caesar* at the Gaiety with himself as Brutus, Sybil as Portia, and ideas for staging, lighting and scenery all taken from the newly published and revolutionary *Art of the Theatre* by Gordon Craig. The result was an uncut, apron-stage production with a permanent set of pillars to avoid long scene changes, and after the first night C. E. Montague published 'a whoop of joy' as his review.

That, however, was a minority report: Manchester in general and Miss Horniman in particular did not care for the 'freakish' ideas of Gordon Craig and cancelled Lewis's plans to do *The Tempest* in similar fashion, whereupon he resigned. Sybil was by now pregnant a third time and feared she might actually give birth during the drama of Lewis's farewell party, at which (according to Russell, who also took a dim view of Craig) Casson laid into his Manchester regulars for their utter lack of interest in Craig and their generally conservative and mean-minded attitude to the theatre.

Then they were off again, Lewis hoping to tour Russia and Germany in search of new theatrical concepts and Sybil soon to have Mary Casson, who was born in London in May 1914. Lewis in the meantime had been offered a temporary assignment directing the first Glasgow repertory theatre, and that took his mind off European travel until the events of 1914 made it clear that if he was to go abroad at all that year it would most probably be in uniform.

Awaiting the birth of Mary, Sybil went back to her piano practice and began to wonder whether what was left of their American savings could be used to start a season under the Cassons' own management that autumn; soon after Mary's birth, though, it became evident that the war would take care of that idea. By now Lewis was back in London doing freelance productions for the Stage Society (whatever economic and critical setbacks were to befall him and his wife across the next half-century in the theatre, unemployment was to remain something which happened to their relatives rather than themselves), and Sybil had taken her new baby and the other two children and a devoted maid-housekeeper down to a cottage at Dymchurch owned by Mrs Thorndike, who was a compulsive property buyer when money allowed. Russell was there too, living in a nearby lifeboat station and writing his eminently successful *Dr Syn*, and the last summer of the peace was, at Dymchurch as elsewhere, an almost idyllic time.

Lewis would come down at weekends from London in his new car (nicknamed 'Hindle Wakes' after one of his most triumphant Manchester productions) and plans went ahead for the first Casson London season in which, said Lewis, Russell would have to be included 'because we need one footler in the company – it keeps the highbrows from getting too high'. Then, however, came August 1914 and Sybil took up her own story at this point in the book she later wrote about Lilian Baylis:

August, 1914: Lewis, my husband, joined the Army. My brother Russell had been a volunteer in the Westminster Dragoons before the war, so he was one of the 'called up' and my younger brother, Frank, left his job with Matheson Lang (in *Mr Wu*) and joined the same regiment, and they were both ordered to Egypt that first awful month. I remember one late afternoon in mid-August, Lewis coming home with a set face, 'Put the children in the pram and let John walk and come out with me.' Up Vauxhall Bridge Road the Casson family trundled. 'I've got to be in this,' he said. 'It's the biggest thing that has happened in our lives, one can't stand apart – it will be a war to finish war forever, I do believe this, so now, what about it?' We planned that I must get back to work as soon as possible – I'd just had my third baby, Mary; she was nearly three months old – and if I couldn't keep things going I must turn into the vicarage and sponge on my parents. We talked it over with them that same evening, and all agreed that Lewis must go. I hated, hated the thought of his fighting Germans, because I'd worked with German musicians, and had such lovely friendships with people of that country and it seemed, when we had music together and in common, a most hideous and wretched betrayal of that friendship. However, the world went mad, and we all went mad, though we did have an aim and a resolve that was good and high-meaning. Lewis enlisted next day, troops kept marching over Vauxhall Bridge past our windows, our little boys John and Christopher dressed up as soldiers, and I played 'Tipperary' and the 'British Grenadiers' on the piano to their marchings, and we all felt thrilled with lumps in our throats and firm resolution in our hearts.

The week of Lewis's departure (at thirty-nine already, he'd had to knock a few years off his age to get into the Army Service Corps) John contracted scarlet fever; so, having sent the rest of the family to her mother at the vicarage, Sybil spent the next seven weeks nursing him through that. Then the children were all reunited for a brief autumn holiday at Dymchurch. While they were there, a letter arrived for Sybil from her old friend and employer Ben Greet:

There's a strange woman running a theatre in the Waterloo Road. You'd find her exciting, Syb, because you're as mad as she is. I'm doing some shows for her with Estelle Stead, so come and join us. *Comedy of Errors* week after next – you play Adriana; I've told them you'd be wonderful, though I don't think you'll really be very good. You always bounce too much – you'd be better as one of the Dromios, or our old pal Luce – still you'll like Lilian Baylis, she's got ideals, and don't go telling her you've not played the part before because she says she wants the best and she's going to get it. God bless you, old Syb, your old friend B.G.

Greet had joined Baylis at the Vic a few weeks earlier, after the collapse there of a Rosina Filippi season of two Shakespeare plays and *The School for Scandal*, but the theatre to which he was now inviting Sybil was not, explains Richard Findlater, the distinguished and widely-acclaimed playhouse it later became. In 1914

the Old Vic had no scene-dock, painting room or flies. There was virtually no wardrobe, and what did exist had to be shared with the opera company. For décor a few stock cloths and props were used over and over again. The two 'star' dressing rooms were little bigger than sedan chairs; many of the cast had to change in the top boxes, the saloon or the wings; and there was no running water. The building had no proper foyer, box-office or stage-door. And the manager had apparently never read a play by Shakespeare or seen one profession-ally performed until Ben Greet brought the Works precariously to life on the stage three times a week.

But, far off the beaten track though the Vic was for actors, critics and audiences alike, Sybil did already know vaguely of Miss Baylis as a visitor to her father's church and as the woman who'd taken over the Vic from Emma Cons, who, in turn, had worked with Sybil's sister-in-law in the social-reform schemes of the East End a few years earlier. Sybil herself recounted her first meeting backstage with Miss Baylis:

I was hailed in friendly fashion. Funny I don't know what she said to me first, as I was a bit taken aback by the coming-on sweep of her, but I remember 'Well, you won't get much pay, but you like the work, don't you, and if your husband's in the army you'd better be doing decent work too – good for you and the child-ren.' Then 'Your father's a priest isn't he? Church and stage – same thing – ought to be!'

And soon Sybil was writing to Russell (now serving in Egypt with their brother Frank) with all the old, buoyant theatrical-schoolgirl enthusiasm that had first characterized her letters home from America a decade ago:

I am rehearsing for a Shakespearian Season at the Old Vic, a theatre near Water-loo Station, run by a perfectly fascinating person called Lilian Baylis, who is the most original woman I've ever met. Simply dying to play her. She'd be a gorgeous part. She's not a bit like a theatrical manager. Much too keen on the 'People' and really the whole thing promises to be great fun. I shall love working for her as she's one of those people who just make you do things. It's rotten pay, but anything is a godsend in these times, and we all eat such a lot. At the Vic we live on coffee and buns. There's not time for anything else, and I find them very nourishing.

In Sybil's first 1914–15 season at the Vic, reports Findlater, Baylis and Ben Greet between them staged a staggering total of sixteen operas and sixteen plays in less than thirty weeks. Sybil herself was getting ten shillings a performance, and after *The Comedy of Errors* she was asked to stay on and tackle her first tragic role in London. It was Lady Macbeth; she was just thirty-two and it was a fair old disaster, as she wrote next morning to Russell:

Played Lady Macbeth last night. Don't laugh. I was too appalling. The critics that I read all said I was unsuited to tragedy as my voice is too light and my features too small. That's rather depressing, isn't it? Never mind, something's got to be done about it, and I mean to jolly well swot until they do think me suitable. Tragedy is awfully difficult, I think, because it's so much larger than real life.

The indomitable Miss Baylis, however, had a way of reducing it to a manageable and familiar scale:

'I think Lady Macbeth is a very easy part for you,' she once told Sybil in rehearsal. 'She loved her husband, and wanted him to get to the top of the tree, and I expect you feel that way too, and if it wasn't that you go to Communion, I dare say you'd do all sorts of wicked things to help Lewis!'

At the end of January Lewis, thoroughly fed up with army life on a base at St Alban's where he'd been allowed to do nothing but cook and learn to drive lorries, was to his delight sent into action in France and Sybil wrote that doing a tragedy like *Macbeth* would relieve her anxieties. By this time their fourth and last child was well on the way, but Sybil played on through the Spring at the Vic, reviving the *Everyman* she'd first done for Greet in America.

Then it was time to gather up the existing children and take them down to Dymchurch to await the new baby. Ann was born on 6 November

Old Vic Company dressed for *Comedy of Errors*, 1916. Sybil Thorndike is standing
by the right side of the arch

and within three days of the birth Sybil awoke to find the implacable Lilian by her bedside: the time had come to start rehearsing *Hamlet*.

'You must give me a little more time,' said Sybil.

'I can't put it off any more,' replied Lilian.

'But Ann was late in arriving.'

'That was her fault, not mine.'

So back to the Vic it was, only to find that she couldn't fit into the Ophelia costumes. 'Don't blame your innocent child,' said Greet, 'you always were tubby, and if I'd got anybody else who could play Ophelia I'd let you do the Player Queen because it doesn't matter if she looks squat.' Playfully, Greet added that she might even repeat her Lucianus, a performance she'd once given for him in America complete with hastily-stuck beard, after which a number of the company had wondered who was the new funny little fat man in their midst.

Lewis was home on leave from truck-driving in France in time to see that Ophelia, and so were Russell and Frank who'd both been in the second Gallipoli landings:

> Some war horrors that one can forget when one reads about them in the news-papers [wrote Sybil] are brought home to one when one sees one's own ... we'd seen Russell and Frank ride away with the regiment looking so jolly and fit ... and now Russell looked an old man – bent nearly double – high spirits nearly gone – and just crawling along.

Lewis took up a commission in the Royal Engineers and he and Frank returned to the Front early in 1916 while Russell, though he could never go back to active service, did recover sufficiently to join his sister at the Vic. Her reviews there were better for Ophelia than for Lady Macbeth, though the business was initially terrible ('£2 in the house and three boys and an orange in the gallery'), since audiences in London were still not used to going to the Vic in its non-operatic half of the week.

But the Baylis band played on, Sybil adding Rosalind and Viola and Imogen to her Vic repertoire (parts she'd only ever played for Greet in America), and critics grudgingly beginning to accept that the Vic (where Tuesday nights were still devoted to 'Illustrated Lectures For Thinking Men'), although it may have lacked glitter and fashionability, was yet fulfilling a useful educational function in that its 'Shakespeare for two pence' ticket policy was introducing large numbers of young people to Shakespeare's work in the broadest possible (in every sense) range of productions.

In August 1916 the Baylis–Greet company travelled to Stratford to fill in for Frank Benson (who was on Red Cross duty) at the festival there celebrating the tercentenary of Shakespeare's death: a photograph taken of the company at the time shows not only Sybil and Russell but also Austin Trevor, Ion Swinley and Robert Atkins, as well, of course, as Greet and Baylis who were in trouble over which of their current leading ladies, Sybil or Nancy Price, should give Stratford her Lady Macbeth. The proprietorial Flower family and the local critics wanted Miss Price. Baylis and B.G. wanted Sybil, and it was Russell who solved the dilemma by suggesting that the two ladies should alternate in the role at matinées and evening performances.

Later in the Stratford season, despite the well-known hatred of Miss Baylis for 'stars', Lilian Braithwaite joined the company for a special matinée of *Henry VIII*, thereby inaugurating a tradition which meant that on subsequent Shakespeare birthdays at the Vic Sybil was to share the stage with the likes of Ellen Terry and Geneviève Ward. But for that year, the Vic company's achievement in staging eleven Shakespeare plays within two Stratford months was hailed locally as 'well-conceived and student-like'; respect and polite interest rather than wild enthusiasm still being the general reaction to the work of Miss Baylis. 'A modicum of pleasure', granted the critic on the local *Herald*.

Back in the Waterloo Road after the festival, they staged an uncut *Hamlet* at the Vic and then started on *King Lear* with Russell in the title role and Sybil – since the war had taken away nearly all the other leading male players – as his Fool. It was, Russell recalled, *Lear* that they were doing on the night of the Waterloo Station air raid:

> I had just reached the passage 'And thou, all-shaking thunder' when there was the most appalling explosion and the Old Vic shook. I was so angry ... that I strode downstage with Sybil at my heels and shaking my fist at the roof of the auditorium shouted, 'Crack Nature's moulds, all *Germans* spill at once!' The audience at the Old Vic are intelligent, quick to seize the slightest point, and their applause swept through the theatre and drowned the sound of the guns, so delighted were they at the aptness of the misquotation and so in sympathy with the sentiment. The applause had barely died away when the Fool capped Lear's remark with 'Here's a night that pities neither wise men nor fool!'

Nor did Miss Baylis have much time for German interruptions. Henry Kendall, a young actor invalided out of the war and taken on at the Vic not because he'd ever played Shakespeare before but because he'd once been at Greet's drama school, recalled that Baylis would go in front of the curtain when there was a raid and say, 'Now, boys and girls, we're not going to let Kaiser Bill interfere with the Vic, and so we shall carry on with this beautiful play, and if you up there on the top shelf would feel any safer you can come down and sit in the stalls – and I won't charge you any extra.'

Later, Sybil wrote, she was on her way to play in *Richard II*:

I was not on until halfway through the show, so was arriving a little late. As I got out of the train in Waterloo Tube Station, I met crowds pouring down the stairs with the Air Raid look on their faces and in their talk too. Lilian was more to be reckoned with, however, than any raid, so up I fought my way to the street. I was stopped by a bobby who said, 'You can't go outside here, my dear, raid's on.'

'I can't help the raid,' I cried, clinging to his brass buttons, 'the curtain's up at the Old Vic, and I shan't be on for my entrance.'

'Old Vic, is it?' he said. 'Oh, I know Miss Baylis; yes, you're right' and, a lull coming in the bomb sounds, he gave me a push into Waterloo Road with a: 'Now run for your life, and if you're killed, don't blame me – blame Her!' I got to the pit door – first door I reached – and found Lilian in a fume and fret. 'Why on earth weren't you in before this?'

'A raid,' I said, 'everybody underground at Waterloo – everything impossible.'

'Raid,' she snorted. 'What's a raid when my curtain's up?'

# 1916-1919

# From Baylis to Cochran

By the winter of 1916 Sybil Thorndike was thirty-four, had been on the stage twelve years, and had in that time been through three distinct theatrical phases: first the barnstorming of America with Greet, then the more socially and politically conscious 'new woman' of the Manchester Gaiety at the time of Miss Horniman and *Jane Clegg* ('it doesn't seem right, somehow, to have a mind and not use it') and now a return to the more mindless, flamboyant, declamatory, expository style of the Baylis–Greet Vic. Her public image, however, was shadowy to the point of invisibility; true, she was becoming known to regular customers in the Waterloo Road (how many women had ever played the Fool in *King Lear* and Hal within the same year?) but critics seldom ventured over Waterloo Bridge and London's more fashionable and influential theatregoers of that time never did. James Agate may have realized (much later) that it was the wartime Vic which made Sybil into a great actress, but few bothered to notice it at the time and, by such contemporary accounts as do exist, much of her work there was still a fair way off greatness.

She herself noted with some pleasure and relief that business at the Vic was slowly but surely improving as the war continued; it was about the only London theatre which hadn't in fact succumbed to the usual wartime demand for musicals and light comedies, and Sybil's father used to encourage his parishioners to make the journey across the Thames – partly out of fanatical loyalty to his elder son and daughter, partly because he'd come to believe along with Sybil and Lilian that the church and Shakespeare were largely synonymous.

After *Lear*, Russell did *Richard III* and then he and Sybil convinced a somewhat dubious Lilian that for Christmas they should do a jolly revue-cum-pantomime satirizing the previous twelve months' work at the Vic and its creators. Sybil, dressed as Miss Baylis, declaimed:

> I'm Lilian Baylis, Lessee:
> And manage this show to perfection:

> Now listen, you bounders, to me,
> Who've worked up this blooming connection:
> A little less free with your jaw:
> And a little more free with your money:
> Monday nights will be better, I'm sure,
> When you realise Shakespeare is funny.
> To roll de roll roll, de rollay,
> The Vic is for ever defying
> These merchants who constantly say
> That the Drama in England is dying.

Later, after the inevitable and ever-urgent appeal for cash, Miss Baylis herself addressed the customers:

I suppose you want to know something of what we are going to do when we re-open. Well, I can't tell you, because I don't know myself, except that unless Monday nights, which continue to be so mucky, get better, we may have to close down, and I don't intend to, so you must all of you pray that they get better. I shall try to get some more good actors cheap, as a lot of the present ones are going. I don't know whether you'll be interested or not to hear that Russell is staying on, as he wants to play Hamlet. He was Matheson Lang's understudy in the part, and played it in South Africa, so he shouldn't be too bad. I know what you're all thinking. That his legs will look funny in black tights. Well, you may laugh, but, do you know, I rather like Russell's legs. Perhaps I shouldn't have said that, as I'm not married.

For this *Hamlet*, Sybil graduated from Ophelia to Gertrude and early in 1917 the company left the Vic to play one-night stands at Holloway and Bethnal Green as well as a short Portsmouth season later; the one-nighters were successful enough to be repeated on a weekly basis on evenings when the Vic stage was otherwise occupied. They also did school matinées which, Sybil decided, were worse than the air raids:

Some kind friend would occasionally provide the little darlings with bags of buns and sweets at the beginning of the performance … a chocolate – a little innocent chocolate – can make such a noise with its wrappings and its clothings, and after the crinkling is done one can almost detect whether it's a nut, or a foul ginger, or the noiseless cream; and teas-teas-teas – and the paying for teas – could any sounds be more ruinous to the performance of a play? Why is this ever allowed? I'd have all bars and teas and foods whipped from the sacred confines … an audience which does not smoke or eat during a performance is more quiet, more attentive and has a greater responsiveness, and there is not a sensitive actor who will not confirm this.

Note those 'sacred confines': the Vic really was a kind of church to Sybil. But away from the theatre the war was claiming more and more lives. Several of the actors with whom Sybil had started at the Vic in 1914 would never play there or anywhere else again, and in the June of 1917, reports John Casson:

I saw my first piece of real life serious drama without any acting. We were in the little sitting room one afternoon and Sybil was kneeling on the floor helping us with some game. Suddenly there was a loud knocking. 'Open the front door, John darling,' said Sybil and I reached up and undid the latch. A tall fat girl stood outside who thrust into my hand an orange envelope saying as she did so 'Telegram for yer mum'. Never as long as I live shall I forget the look of abject terror on Sybil's face as she tore open the telegram. In those days of long casualty lists telegrams were frequent and horrifying, and Sybil fully expected to read that Lewis had been killed in action. But as she read she gave a great sigh of relief and said, 'Thank God, he's wounded.' At seven years old I was astonished that she should be so pleased to know that Lewis was wounded, until she told me that this would probably mean he would be coming home soon.

When Lewis did come home he brought with him a piece of shrapnel embedded in his shoulder and the award of a Military Cross for his courage in carrying cylinders of phosgene out into no-man's-land. But a month or two later the news was very much worse: an army chaplain came to tell Sybil that her brother Frank had been shot down in action. Remembering that his last performance at the Vic had been as Young Siward in *Macbeth*, they put under his name on the family grave at Aylesford:

> He paid a soldier's debt
> He only lived but till he was a man
> The which no sooner had his prowess confirmed
> In the unshrinking station where he fought
> But like a man he died.
> .... Why then, God's soldier be he!

Canon Thorndike told the family that Frank had died nobly and gloriously in the service of his country, but the shock of his younger son's sudden death was considerable and may well have hastened his own end which came, also suddenly, during a service in his own church on 9 December of that year.

Sybil, stunned by this double blow to her close-knit family life, ploughed on through the winter season at the Vic from *King John* to the

annual revue. By now she was playing several male parts, since the company was still decimated by war: apart from the Fool and Hal, both Ferdinand in *The Tempest* and Launcelot Gobbo in *The Merchant* were also
within her repertoire although, sadly, there exists very little critical evidence of what she was like at any of them. Even so regular, dedicated
and loyal a theatregoer as W. A. Darlington (soon to become an almost
lifelong drama critic on the *Daily Telegraph*) had to admit that he seldom
went near the Vic at this time:

> I was a soldier on leave, taking his girl out to a dinner and a show, but in
> spite of my pre-war conversion to Shakespeare and my acquaintance, now con-
> siderable, with his text, I never thought to visit the Old Vic ... if there was a
> straight play to be seen we saw it; if not, we went to the revues and took our
> crude enjoyment with the rest.

Now that Lewis was invalided home from the war and picking up,
albeit slowly, the threads of his own career in the commercial theatre,
he was eager for Sybil to escape the ten-shillings-a-show anonymity of
the Vic and start making her name in the West End. So too was Miss
Baylis, though for rather different reasons. In Shakespeare, as she openly
and bluntly put it backstage, Sybil was 'getting stale'. Happily for everyone concerned, in early 1918 the company also had a revival of *The School
for Scandal* in the repertoire with Sybil as Lady Teazle. In the audience
for that, one night, was the impresario Charles Blake Cochran who had
also seen Sybil in a Christmas revue-sketch called *Spooks*, which was, not
altogether surprisingly, a parody of *Ghosts*. Thinking he might have
spotted a new comedienne, Cochran offered Sybil a month at the London
Pavilion supporting an eccentric French comedian called Leon Morton
on a variety bill. Baylis was almost embarrassingly eager to let her
go:

> Like a mother she pushed me from a nest where I was getting comfortable
> and feeling safe. 'Out you go,' she'd say in so many words. 'The Vic wants grow-
> ing people. The Vic wants new blood. No one who is settling down is any use
> to a growing theatre. Out you go and learn something new somewhere else.
> Come back to us when you've learnt some more.'

So Sybil left the Vic, not of course forever (she was back in 1919 with
matinées of *The Trojan Women* and then in much later seasons with
the company) but at the end of the longest uninterrupted stay she was
ever to have there. Yet the Vic was to remain her spiritual home for
the rest of a long life, and it was wonderfully if sadly fitting that her

last public appearance should have been in the audience there a few weeks before her death, on the occasion of the National Theatre Company's departure from the Waterloo Road to their palatial new premises on the South Bank.

On that memorable night of *A Tribute to the Lady* in February 1976, with Sybil in the stalls and Susan Fleetwood playing her on the stage while Peggy Ashcroft played Lilian, all the old Baylis stories were recalled: how she used to sizzle steaks and onions in the wings during the last act of *As You Like It*, how she would pray 'Dear God, send me some good actors and send them cheap', and how on one occasion an actor demanding a rise watched her leave the room, only to return a few minutes later murmuring 'Sorry, dear, God says No.' Sybil herself had earlier recalled trying to get through a *Macbeth* matinée with Baylis and Robert Atkins squabbling bitterly and so audibly in the wings that Russell got a terribly unwanted laugh on the line 'How is't with me when every noise appals me?'

But thrilled though Baylis was to see Sybil leave the nest, she was not entirely sure about the new company her old friend had fallen into; going backstage at the Pavilion after Sybil's first night in the Morton sketch she told her:

Nice to see you wearing such a pretty frock – it's good for you. I think the Frenchman [Morton] is very vulgar and rather like the gutter boys of the New Cut, but he's no worse than Shakespeare, and anyway he makes us all laugh and enjoy the gutter more than we should if left to ourselves, and he's got a very sweet face, and do you think he's a good Christian, Syb? Such a lot of Frenchmen are!

Baylis was to remain a friend, adviser, confidante and employer to the Thorndike family for several years to come, even encouraging Sybil's mother to take to the boards after her husband's death. Mrs Thorndike refrained, but the two ageing ladies shared hair-raising journeys around London in Lilian's car, from which Miss Baylis would lean out of the driving seat and shout to amazed pedestrians and policemen, 'Out of my way! I've got Sybil Thorndike's mother in the car so get out of the way, you bounders! She plays Saint Joan and if you don't know that, more silly you! Out of the way!'

But Saint Joan was still five years off, and in the meantime Cochran was not at all sure about the talent he had acquired from the Vic; after a month with Morton at the Pavilion, he moved Sybil to the New Oxford

in a tragic war sketch called *The Kiddies in the Ruins* which formed part
of a curious but highly successful World War I nostalgia show called *The
Better 'Ole*. Later he wrote of Sybil in one of his autobiographies: 'Her
performance at the Oxford was a little too restless. She had at that time
a number of mannerisms, and lacked repose. Her voice also lacked flexibility. But she was a conscientious artist, and a charming woman to be
associated with.'

Sybil, all too conscious that her voice not only 'lacked flexibility' but
was in imminent danger of collapsing once again, as it had in America,
now went to Elsie Fogerty for vocal coaching. But the job at the New
Oxford only lasted a month or so, and from the time of that brief – some
might say bizarre – double introduction to Cochran's commercial-theatre
world until the Christmas which followed it, Sybil had to exist profession-
ally on occasional two-guinea jobs from the Stage Society. Lewis was
equally hard up for work at the end of 1918, though soon afterwards he
got Le Bret in Robert Loraine's all-serviceman production of *Cyrano de
Bergerac*, which saw them through much of the next year. Sybil meanwhile got a job understudying Madge Titheradge in *The Night Watch*
and then had the good fortune to meet up again with Ellen Terry's
daughter, Edith Craig, who was running the Pioneer Players. Thirty years
later, Sybil wrote of her various debts to Edy:

> It was at the Old Vic from 1914 that I began to know her. . . . I can see Edy
> now, sitting in the wings and having to reintroduce us to Ellen Terry who never
> really remembered any of us. Edy said Ellen never recalled my name but always
> said, 'You know – that big girl' which slightly hurt my pride, because as I wasn't
> tall I knew it must have referred to my rather square bounciness, as was proved
> afterwards by Edy saying to me so frequently, 'Keep still – don't flounce and
> bounce' . . . it was during her Pioneer Theatre days that I came under her direc-
> tion. The most memorable was her production of *The Hostage*. She cast me for
> the part of Sygne . . . and this proved to be one of my biggest spiritual experiences
> in the theatre.

*The Hostage* was not, needless to add, the Behan creation but instead
a poetic drama by Claudel set in a remote Cistercian Abbey during Napoleon's Russian campaign, and Sybil's was the only female part. It won
her high praise from *The Times* ('we had never before seen Miss Thorndike act with so much passion, so much sensitiveness, such a flow of
agonising beauty'). J. C. Trewin no doubt accurately summarized the
opinion of critics who saw her when he wrote later of her 'compelling
attack, the fierceness with which she thought, felt, communicated' but

added the now-familiar rider about her voice being 'not yet right'. Another critic was alert to Sybil's tendency to go over the top even in subdued dramas: 'Miss Thorndike will be a great actress,' he wrote, 'so long as she learns to keep her hands beneath her shoulders.'

## 1919-1922

# The Greeks and Grand Guignol

The reviews which Sybil got for that one Sunday night performance of *The Hostage* were not only the best she'd yet had but also the best-displayed; overnight she had completed the crossing of Waterloo Bridge back into the heartland of the West End, not just for a supporting role on a Cochran variety bill but now for a major dramatic part which suddenly awoke the popular press to her presence in their theatrical midst. But the last year at the Vic, the year of Lewis's return from the Front, had not been an especially easy one:

I'd been getting 'separation allowance' from Lewis, but it didn't make things much better. I did have two darling girls from father's village who came and worked for me, but I couldn't always pay them because with only ten shillings a show at the Vic that came to three pounds ten a week which was pretty stiff with a family of four children. ... I also had a bit of voice trouble and I had to go and get some more help from Elsie Fogerty whom I'd known ever since I'd married Lewis. 'He's got the best voice in the English theatre,' she told me then, 'I hope you're worthy of it.' Somehow I don't believe she thought I was, but later she did help me a lot. ... I was overworking, rushing back and forth to the Vic and I couldn't take taxis because I didn't have the money. I was using my voice wrongly, overstraining it, trying to push too hard. ... Fogerty got me through difficult times and I never had to be off at all. ... She went through the whole thing of breathing, and relaxing was one of the first things she taught me. She had a wonderful way of focussing the voice and helping you to get all the notes.

And now, with Lewis going into the Loraine *Cyrano* and Sybil armed with her *Hostage* reviews, came at last the chance for the Cassons to make a little money. First Leon M. Lion gave Sybil forty pounds a week for replacing the ailing Ethel Irving in *The Chinese Puzzle* at the New Theatre, and then, in September 1919, she got the lead in one of the last great Drury Lane melodramas, *The Great Day*. These were solid West End commercial jobs and she was glad of them after so long in the artistic wilderness over the bridge, though neither show did much to enhance her reputation among the critics.

In the meantime, however, Lewis had been asked to provide a special matinée in Oxford as part of the 'No More War' pacifist symposium to be held there. Lewis had been retrospectively appalled by the First War and by his own part in it (despite the fact that this had earned him an MC from a grateful George V) and the chance to celebrate the coming of the League of Nations, together with its promise of everlasting peace, was one he grabbed eagerly. The play to do, he decided, would be Gilbert Murray's adaptation of *The Trojan Women* with its awful warnings about war ('Would ye be wise, ye cities, fly from war') and to help him set it up he got Bruce Winston, with whom he'd been sharing a *Cyrano* dressing-room, to design the costumes.

At first Sybil was too involved at Drury Lane to play any part, and Hecuba went to Evelyn Walsh Hall; later in the autumn, though, Lewis was asked to re-stage his production for one performance at the Alhambra and now, in London one afternoon, Sybil was able to take it on:

The music [she told Elizabeth Sprigge] was thrilling; I can hear now those twelve splendid trumpet chords which opened the performance, and I felt that to play Hecuba was the most wonderful thing that could happen to me. There were shouts at the end for 'Author!' louder than I have ever heard, and Gilbert Murray came up on to the stage. 'The author is not here,' he said. 'He has been dead for many centuries but I am sure he will be gratified by your reception of his great tragedy.'

Lewis directed and played Poseidon and Talthybius, and for the *Daily Express* Archibald Haddon, one of Sybil's earliest and staunchest supporters, wrote that 'the tragedy is 2,334 years old but its message is eternal and its note of human grief sounded as poignantly as it did in the Grecian theatre centuries before Christ'. Of Sybil he added that 'the actress seemed born for Hecuba and her transition from the role to that of the girl-heroine at Drury Lane on the evening of the same day constituted almost a freakish exhibition of versatility'.

Sybil herself was not convinced, and nor was Lewis. Russell found her in the dressing-room:

She was terribly depressed after the first show and I got quite huffy with her, as I thought for the first time in her life she was posing; but it wasn't that at all, it was just Lewis, who has the knack of looking like a mute at a funeral when everyone else is happy. 'He depresses me dreadfully,' wailed Sybil, chucking her

Hecuba roles at her face in the mirror. 'He says I'm not the least bit suited to Hecuba – blast her – and I know it, so what does he want to rub it in for? He says I haven't got her face or her voice, and he's quite right and that's the stinking part of it. I loathe the way I play her more than he does, but I will play her one day if it's only to say "Sucks" to Lewis.'

But whatever Lewis's misgivings, the press reaction meant that her performance could clearly not be allowed to disappear after a single afternoon at the Alhambra; and soon afterwards, with Sybil still appearing every evening in the melodrama at Drury Lane, the faithful Miss Baylis offered them the Vic for four special matinées of *The Trojan Women*. These were immediately sold out and, spurred by their success, Casson and Norman V. Norman (now in partnership) approached Charles Gulliver at the Holborn Empire and asked if they could have his music hall for special Greek-drama matinées, something which no West End management was at that time prepared to contemplate: this was after all the time when, as Darlington once said, the commercial theatre was largely in the managerial hands of 'speculative tradesmen'.

To his everlasting credit Gulliver (who'd never been to the Vic, but had a deep and spiritual horror of any theatre of his being dark, even in the afternoons) let them into the Empire at a generous rental and after a few weeks Casson had a clear profit of two hundred pounds. To this he and Winston added a further thousand pounds borrowed from Lord Howard de Walden and (as Sybil's melodrama at the Lane had at last reached the end of its run) they extended their lease at Holborn – where Harry Tate's bicycling sketch was now the evening attraction – so that they were entirely responsible for all matinées there.

To *The Trojan Women* they added Gilbert Murray's new translation of *Medea* and a revival of Shaw's *Candida* with Sybil in each of the title roles and Lewis directing and playing the Messenger and Morrell. It was at these matinées that W. A. Darlington first began to consider not only Sybil's present achievements but also her general standing in the London theatre at the beginning of 1920:

These performances were nothing short of a revelation to me. They made me realize, without ambiguity, what I had hitherto known only subconsciously, that we now had two different kinds of audience. If acting so powerful, so full of passion and beauty, so deeply moving as that of Miss Thorndike in Greek tragedy was being neglected by the great majority even of the more enlightened play-goers, it must be because these playgoers did not want to be moved in that way. To use a word which had not then passed into ordinary language, they were

ABOVE As Hucuba in *The Trojan Women* with her son, Christopher Casson, at the Holborn Empire, December 1919

ABOVE RIGHT As Medea, Holborn Empire, March 1920

RIGHT On the beach at Dymchurch, August 1921: Lewis and Sybil with (*from the left*) Mary, Ann, John and Christopher

allergic to Miss Thorndike's methods: they could react only to the restrained
playing of actors like du Maurier. . . . Candida caused no special stir – there were
a dozen good actresses who might have played that part equally well – but the
effect of the two Greek performances was explosive. None of the critics had seen
tragic performances of this calibre since the war, and I myself, only three months
a critic and with my playgoing experience still lopsided, had never seen tragic
acting of this calibre in my life before. The press notices were of a nature to
give the actress a star's prestige overnight, though they could not give her a
star's following . . . those two performances, but particularly that of Hecuba in
*The Trojan Women*, still glow in my memory. . . . I believe they had a true
tragic grandeur. . . .

Drawn by unanimously enthusiastic notices, the small playgoing public which
liked heroic-scale acting flocked to the Holborn Empire and made that matinée
season, with its appointed limits, a complete success. The larger public was interested but remained aloof. This new actress was evidently something out of the
common, but one could hardly go to see her while she was appearing in those
absurd Greek things. . . . Yet I believe she originally had it in her, given a quicker
rise and a more sympathetic and theatre-wise public, to become something she
did not quite attain to – a great, a really great tragic actress. I saw her touch
greatness, certainly as Hecuba, perhaps as Medea, and I hoped that these achievements were the prelude to others greater still – but they were not, they were
her peak. Never again did I experience with her that sense of surrender which
is the involuntary tribute that one pays to emotional acting at its highest pitch.

The success of those Holborn matinées was to be short-lived; in Russell's view the Casson management lost its head by adding to the two
Greek plays and *Candida* a new drama called *Tom Trouble* which, true
to its awful title, lost them all the money they had made on the earlier
two. The Holborn season therefore came to an abrupt halt in May 1920
and once again, neither for the first time nor for the last, the Cassons were
without a theatre or visible means of support though not, as ever, for
very long.

They both went into a thriller at the St James's called *The Mystery of
the Yellow Room* in which Sybil was, according to her brother, sensational
in the big trial scene despite the fact that, such was its complexity, she
never managed to discover who in it was being tried or for what. An
old family friend, Father Olivier, brought his thirteen-year-old son
Laurence to this play as his introduction to the theatre and the Cassons,
and later Sybil (whose tireless habit it always was to do Sunday night
shows during a long run) went back to Edy Craig's Pioneer Players to
do a French play called *Carnaval des Enfants*. Also in the cast was a youngish

Edith Evans, who half a century later declined to recall anything about it except that she and Sybil had managed to get on 'quite well' together, that Sybil had 'marvellous eyes set in a perfect forehead', and that she also seemed to have a curiously large number of relatives in the business.

But, as Darlington had realized, occasional highbrow Sunday night specials and a series of Greek matinées, however startlingly impressive (a young Philip Hope-Wallace, seeing the Greek double, knew he was 'in the presence of greatness'), was not going to win Sybil a wide popular following. For that, something else was needed, and it emerged in the autumn of 1920 via José Levy who was then in control of the Little Theatre in John (Adam) Street, Adelphi. During a stay in Paris he had seen and been hugely impressed by the Grand Guignol seasons there, which were sets of short plays, some comic but most tragic, massively overacted and depending for their effects on a series of spine-chillingly horrific and deathly climaxes of a kind later to become indelibly associated with the film output of Hammer Studios.

There were some doubts among Levy's colleagues and friends about whether London would ever take to Grand Guignol (the French, thought Russell, were an emotional race, whereas the English were too 'roast-beefy and foggy' to accept something so temperamental), but Levy was undeterred. Looking, perhaps, for the most flamboyant actors around the West End in 1920 he rapidly settled on a company led by Sybil and Russell and including, more surprisingly, Lewis as chief director and co-star, brought in presumably to keep the proceedings under some sort of artistic control.

For fully two years at the Little Theatre the three of them (together with the likes of Athene Seyler, Nicholas Hannen, Ian Fleming and Dorothy Minto) were gainfully employed scaring the living daylights out of their customers in plays with titles such as *The Hound of Death*, *The Kill*, *De Mortuis* or simply *Fear*. In these, Sybil was variously strangled, asphyxiated, dismembered, locked in trunks, crushed under falling ceilings or merely poisoned; in others she herself strangled or dismembered Russell, and a number of London playgoers and critics took a very dim view indeed of the proceedings. Several stormed out in mid-act, one old gentleman was sick on the mat in the foyer, and reviews in the national press were routinely headlined 'horrible', 'brutal' and 'bestial'.

In *When the Pie was Opened* a one-armed guest at dinner with Sybil discovered the whereabouts of his other arm, and in *The Old Ladies*, the play which caused the most furore of all, Sybil had her eyes gouged out by the knitting needles of the crazed fellow inmates of an asylum. There was also a play about someone eaten alive by werewolves, of which many felt the most interesting and disturbing aspect was the noise Lewis made offstage as the wolves. All in all it was a cheerful time, and if it did not win for Sybil the kind of glowing reviews she had received for the Greek dramas, it did at last bring her name and her work to an infinitely wider public. What is more, as she told Elizabeth Sprigge, she had herself a ball:

For me, playing terrible parts is really rather like a Confessional, only I find it more satisfying. I went to Confession in the Church regularly for years, then I had to give it up because it was making me niggling in myself – it wasn't symbolic enough for me. I can get things out of me much better in the theatre ... you're right outside your own body. I discussed this sense of release I got when I was in Guignol with a doctor once, and he quite understood, but thought it was rather hard luck on the audience to work all that off on them.

Her family were not so sure, though Sybil was determined that they should all see her at her most ghoulish. John recalls her promising: 'There'll be lots of exciting murders and crimes and all sorts of terribly quirky things and everyone will be terrified ... it'll be just like the plays Russell and I used to do in the attic when we were children. Lots of blood and agony ... but you like being frightened a bit, don't you? It's such fun.'

Sybil remained convinced that a little horror was good for everyone:

There were some things I had awful nightmares about all my life, and I wouldn't have dared to go to a psychoanalyst in case he said something dreadful to me. But during the Grand Guignol time I never had a single nightmare ... I would come out feeling clean, too – well, fairly clean anyway. After *Medea* it was the same. My children used to say I was never so angelic and sweet-tempered as I was after Medea, I'd got rid of all my tempers and all the people I'd wanted to murder I'd murdered in the play, and all the terrible rages had been raged – and I came out pure like a whitewashed lamb!

There were, of course, occasionally less horrific diversions during those Guignol years. Sybil was invited to Paris to play her Lady Macbeth in a special performance given to celebrate the eventual signing of the Peace Treaty. Macbeth was played by the American James Hackett (who got the Legion of Honour for it) but such other English stalwarts as Miles Malleson and Leslie Faber were also in the cast, and so too, rather more surprisingly, was the poet John Drinkwater as Banquo. Sybil was allowed

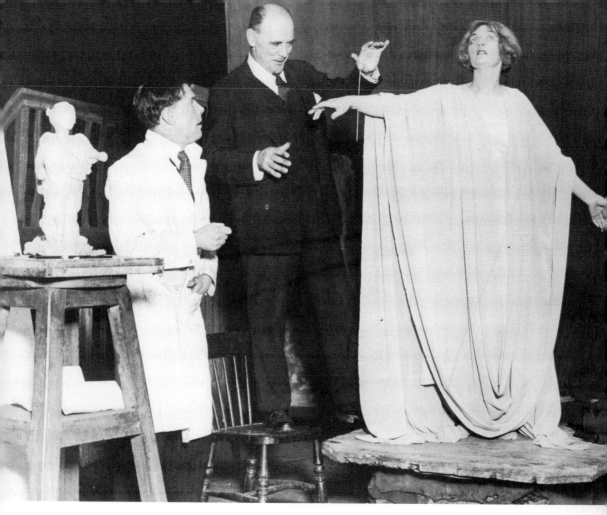

With Lewis Casson and
Lawrence Anderson in *The
Medium*, Grand Guignol as seen
at the London Palladium in
1931

Depicting 'Fear!' in *The Person
Unknown*, Grand Guignol
season, Little Theatre, 1920–22

by Edy Craig to wear all the original Ellen Terry costumes and the whole affair was widely acclaimed, while back home at the Little Theatre three separate actresses had to be found to take over Sybil's roles in the Guignol.

Another diversion at this time was Sybil's entry into films, a medium she never much cared for even after the arrival of sound. During 1921–2 she made a series of silent shorts including *Moth and Rust* and some depicting 'tense moments from the classics' including a scene as Lady Deadlock from *Bleak House* and one as Esmeralda from *The Hunchback of Notre Dame*. Sadly most of these have now disappeared forever from the archives, though Russell remembered them opening at a trade show during which Sybil walked out murmuring that to see herself on the screen made her lose all interest in her own personality. She was not to return to films until *Dawn*, the controversial film about Edith Cavell made in 1928.

# 1922-1923

## 'I have found my Joan'

Towards the end of their two-year stint in Grand Guignol, the Cassons again got the chance to set up on their own in management. It came this time from the actress Mary Moore, widow of Sir Charles Wyndham, who was then in sole charge of the New Theatre in St Martin's Lane (later renamed the Albery in memory of her son Bronson). She had seen Sybil playing Katharine of Aragon in a charity production of *Henry VIII*, one of the special matinées that were still very much a part of the indefatigable Cassons' routine; during the Guignol years Sybil had also done a chilling Mother Sawyer in *The Witch of Edmonton* (again with Edith Evans) for the Stage Society, and Evadne in *The Maid's Tragedy* for the Phoenix Society during which, said Agate, she offered 'enough bitter satirical largesse to defray the comic expenditure of half the fashionable actresses in London'. In other words, she was over the top again.

But her Katharine was by all accounts very impressive indeed, and on the strength of it Lady Wyndham offered her and Lewis a season at the New Theatre, adding generously that if it went economically adrift she would sort out the debts. Leslie Faber was chosen to be their leading man, and they opened with a revival of St John Ervine's ever-popular *Jane Clegg*, following it up with Henri Bataille's *Scandal*, which also did good business – so good that they were able also to revive the *Medea* matinées.

Next came the play which more than any other was to affect Sybil's future career in the theatre: *The Cenci*. Although a hundred years had now passed since Shelley's death, and the play was off the banned list, the Cassons thought it right to get special permission from the Lord Chamberlain to stage Shelley's drama of incest. Permission granted (largely perhaps because a month or two earlier Pirandello's *Six Characters in Search of an Author* had been seen in London without noticeably harmful effect), they opened *The Cenci* at the New Theatre on 13 November 1922 to a generally ecstatic press though Agate (as often where Sybil was concerned) had his doubts. About her performance he said that, while admiring its conveyance of moral grandeur, he 'would as soon think of being sorry for a marble statue as of being sorry for Sybil'. The problem was, in his view, her over-exposure to the more distant classics: 'let her not look upon masterpieces only', he wrote, and for the rest of her career it's fair to say that she took him at his word almost too often.

Lewis himself played the Judge in his own production – a 'strange, un-realistic and symbolic' one according to Sybil. The first night programme indicates that it was staged under the joint management of Sybil and Mary Moore, and that the current going price for 'new two-seater roadsters' was just two hundred and sixty pounds. The following morning, 14 November, *The Times* published its notice alongside the announcement that Marconi broadcasting was officially authorized to begin that day. Of Sybil in *The Cenci*, *The Times* thought that her acting 'falters while terror possesses Beatrice, yet attains a strength and beauty which we have not before seen in it when the fatal decision [to revenge] is once taken. Miss Thorndike converts Beatrice into a New Woman, and gives to her very hardness a majesty that draws all the spirits of tragedy to her feet.'

In the *New Statesman* that week, Maurice Baring was equally enthusias-tic: 'When she spoke the final lines it was clear that not only was Shelley a great poet and that we had lost in him a great dramatist, but that we had found in Miss Thorndike a tragic actress.' The celebrated *Cenci* trial scene was generally reckoned to exhibit Sybil at her current best, and it led to the most important single opportunity of her entire career: return-ing home after seeing one of the matinées, Bernard Shaw said simply to his wife, 'I have found my Joan.'

But the Shaw play was two more years in the making. In the meantime the Cassons took a winter holiday in Italy: 'the greatest treat of my life', said Sybil and meant it, though the phrase was to be repeated at the end of almost every one of her subsequent overseas visits. This was the first holiday that she and Lewis had been able to take together since the out-break of war eight years earlier, and at the suggestion of Robert Farquhar-son, their leading man from *The Cenci*, they went first to Rapallo where they met the pioneer stage designer Gordon Craig and outlined with him a production of *Macbeth* which all three were keen to do and never did, largely because they could not find a suitable theatre. This minor diffi-culty, however, did not deter Craig from arriving in London some weeks later, presenting his designs to Casson and then charging him for them – a bill which soured what might otherwise have been a long and produc-tive friendship.

Photographed by E. O. Hoppé in 1922

Unable to stage *Macbeth* the Cassons instead renewed their alliance with the Albery family, taking the Criterion in partnership with Bronson and staging *Advertising April*, an altogether forgettable (and now forgotten) but at the time highly successful light comedy satirizing that new phenomenon, the film star, and written by two drama critics of the time, Herbert Farjeon and Horace Horsnell. Its subtitle was *The Girl who Made the Sunshine Jealous*, and Sybil – in one of the less plausible casting assignments of a long and varied career – played her. Some flavour of the piece may be gathered from the subsequent memoirs of Mr Horsnell who, whimsical to the last, wrote his autobiography in Augustan couplets:

> Their saucy satire has a movie theme:
> Good Business crowns creation's happy Dream:
> The Tragic Muse (who ne'er leaves things half done)
> Ingenious Sybil! finds their play good fun;
> And (Hecuba persuaded from her woes)
> She takes the stage in frills and furbelows.
> April's début (hidden from public sight)
> Her authors watch with unalloyed delight.

*Advertising April* lasted five months in London and nearly as long again on the road, and although Russell reports a certain unrest among her classically-minded fans who felt she should 'stick to tragedy', the show was a considerably greater success than the *Cymbeline* with which the Cassons followed it in London. She had already played Imogen, of course, at the Vic, and earlier in the same year there had been a controversial modern-dress production by Ayliff at Birmingham. Now, however, Sybil and Lewis brought the play to the New Theatre and Agate was hugely unimpressed: 'Miss Thorndike gives the impression of having swallowed the character at one gulp and of looking around the stage for something with which to be effective.' 'Too much intellect,' added another critic dismissively, 'too little charm.'

As a result the Albery–Casson management got barely a month out of *Cymbeline* and used up on it almost all the proceeds from *April*. Shaw was amazed that anyone troubled to see it at all, commenting that 'the English are a strange people who return to London in the autumn after killing chickens on the moors of Scotland to enjoy themselves at the theatre, watching a young woman waking up beside the headless body of her fiancé', while J. C. Trewin has described it as 'an odd and lovely collision of the Renaissance with Snow White and Lear's Britain'.

ABOVE LEFT As Beatrice in Shelley's *The Cenci* with Lawrence Anderson as Giacomo, New Theatre, November 1922. Bernard Shaw, leaving the theatre: 'I have found my Joan.'

ABOVE RIGHT As April Mawne in *Advertising April*, Criterion Theatre, January 1923: 'Their saucy satire has a movie theme.'

Sybil Thorndike in the 1920s.

Clearly however it was not going to do, and within three weeks of opening night the Cassons had put into rehearsal a nine-year-old (but unseen
outside New York) play by Henry Arthur Jones who, alongside Pinero,
had pioneered the well-made play of the 1880s and 1890s in London.

The Lie was a melodramatic tale of two sisters, both in love with the
same man, one of whom has an illegitimate baby but lets the man believe
the other to be the child's mother; before he can discover the truth she
marries him, leaving the first sister with the consolation of her love for
the child. Sybil had a splendid moment all but throttling the faithless rela-
tive and calling out, as the second act curtain fell, 'Judas Sister!', a cry
which her son John took to be an appeal for a jute assister, whatever that
might be. But Jones himself was delighted with her, the production and
its reception. In dedicating the play to Sybil he recalled that he had begun
writing it in 1913 while searching the South of France for the villa where
the great Rachel was supposed to have died:

My searchings were in vain. What does that matter? Rachel is dead, but you
are alive. I have had many roaring receptions of applause from English first-
nighters, but none of them has approached the thundering welcome they gave
me when, under the shelter of your wing, myself moved by the inflaming sweep
of your acting, I stood beside you to acknowledge the prolonged acclamations
that greeted us on the 13th October 1923.

How lucky I was, after six years' absence from the London theatre, to return
to it in such company as yours! What words of gratitude will fitly express my
debt to you? What words of praise can I choose to describe the patient tenderness
of your quiet early scenes, swelling into stronger but still reserved and self-
contained emotion, startled at last into this poignant and terrific fury of your great
tragic abandonment? Take all the dictionaries, and pick out of them all their
superlatives of eulogy, and I will multiply them again and again.

The Lie carried Sybil into 1924, and at the beginning of that year she
also began doing matinées of Gruach, Gordon Bottomley's verse play
about the young Lady Macbeth. Basil Dean directed her in this (with Mal-
colm Keen as Macbeth) and broke her at last of her habit of indicating
high emotion by going up on tiptoe. He was however still not happy
with the production: 'Sybil's performance as Gruach gave high promise
of a future Lady Macbeth, but what should have been a joyous vindication
of our poets' faith in poetic drama turned out to be a dull and lifeless
performance.'

Meanwhile The Lie, despite or rather because of its great success, had
become a millstone around Sybil's neck; for Shaw was eager to get on

with *Saint Joan* in London. The general view has always been that the formal canonization of Joan in 1920 had put the idea of such a play into Mrs Shaw's head and thence into his, but from a very much earlier date it is evident that the idea was Shaw's alone. In September 1913 he had found himself in Orleans on a motoring holiday and had written from there a series of postcards to that most famous of all his correspondents, Mrs Patrick Campbell:

Strangely enough I have never been in Orleans before, though I have been all over the Joan of Arc country. ... I shall do a Joan play some day, beginning with the sweeping up of the cinders and orange peel *after* her martyrdom, and going on with Joan's arrival in heaven. I should have God about to damn the English for their share in her betrayal and Joan producing an end of burnt stick in arrest of Judgement. 'What's that? Is it one of the faggots?' says God. 'No,' says Joan, 'it's what is left of the two sticks a common English soldier tied together and gave me as I went to the stake; for they wouldn't even give me a crucifix; and you cannot damn the common people of England, represented by that soldier, because a poor cowardly riff-raff of barons and bishops were too futile to resist the devil.' That soldier is the only redeeming figure in the whole business. English literature must be saved (by an Irishman, as usual) from the disgrace of having nothing to show concerning Joan except the piffling libel in *Henry VI*, which reminds me that one of my scenes will be Voltaire and Shakespeare running down bye streets in heaven to avoid meeting Joan. Would you like to play Joan and come in on horseback in armour and fight innumerable supers?

The idea of a play about Joan (though it apparently didn't appeal to Mrs Pat, and though Shaw's final draft was bereft of scenes featuring Voltaire and Shakespeare in heaven) had thus been in existence for a decade before 1924, and it had also occurred to Sybil as a likely vehicle for herself long before she knew of Shaw's interest. 'A woman who argues about everything like blazes', wrote Agate later, 'was bound to be attracted to a woman who ends in blazes', and by 1923 Lewis and Sybil had commissioned their friend the poet Laurence Binyon to write a play about the Maid. Binyon was already well into his version when, during the run of *The Lie*, the Cassons heard of Shaw's play and wrote to him in some consternation asking what they should do. Shaw was in no doubt: 'Sybil is to play my Joan; let someone else play Binyon's.' George Bernard Shaw had, he said, thought to warn off Masefield and Drinkwater; somehow he'd forgotten about Binyon, though the latter gracefully withdrew from the conflict.

With the Shavian version completed at last, Sybil and Lewis were summoned to hear the author read it. The next day Sybil wrote to her son John:

We had the most wonderful day yesterday. We went to lunch with Mr and Mrs Bernard Shaw at their house in Ayot St Lawrence just north of London. He wanted to read us the play he has just finished about Joan of Arc. And so Daddy and I drove down in the morning and got there about half-past twelve. We had a lovely lunch – chicken for us and all sorts of funny-looking things for him because he's a vegetarian – and then he took us into a nice comfy sitting room and we all sat down in armchairs. Then he began to read us the play. He read it beautifully – he ought to have been an actor really, and from the moment he started we couldn't move! You know how I've always longed to play Joan of Arc and I'd been having the most awful quirks that I wouldn't like the Joan he'd written. But we needn't have worried. It's the most marvellous play and we're so excited we don't know what to do. He says that he wants us to do it as soon as possible and we're going to as soon as the silly old *Lie* is finished. No time for more, Darling, I must fly! Your tin of petit-beurre biscuits is in the post.

The reading (also attended by Bronson Albery, who was still in management with the Cassons, and by Shaw's friend Cherry-Garrard who'd been with Scott to the South Pole) was indeed such a success that, talking to me in her Chelsea flat almost exactly half a century later, Sybil was able to re-enact it:

When Shaw read the first act, I nearly jumped out of my skin: I thought 'but this is marvellous'. When he started with 'No eggs! No eggs! Thousand thunders, man, what do you mean by no eggs?' I thought to myself 'this is going to be St Joan?' But when he got to 'And there will be no eggs while the Maid is at the door' and Baudricourt said, 'Maid? What Maid? D'you mean to say that girl I told you to send back is still there?' I knew we'd got it, though I thought Shaw could never live up to that first scene. When he did, I nearly died: and then he read on and got to 'How long, O Lord, how long' and I shall never forget how he did it. He was a marvellous actor, you know: very big-size and so daring and true. When he got to the end of the Loire scene where the wind changes, Shaw said, 'Well, that's all flapdoodle but now the real play starts' and he went into the tent scene with Warwick. When it came to the Epilogue Lewis and I were in tears, though I could tell that Albery wasn't too keen: other people all thought the play could do without an Epilogue, but Shaw said you had to show what would happen if Joan came back into the modern world and it was all just the same.

# St Sybil and St Bernard

The first night of *Saint Joan* was still a long way off, however; throughout the winter of 1923 Sybil continued to play in *The Lie* and to do matinées of *Gruach* while Shaw, eager to get his play staged sooner rather than later, gave it to the New York Theatre Guild with whom he had a contract. Their first performance was on 28 December with Winifred Lenihan creating the role of Joan, Morris Carnovsky as La Hire and Jo Mielziner (later to become America's most distinguished stage designer) as the Page. Reviews were generally good, though more respectful than ecstatic.

By February 1924 the Cassons had managed to bring *The Lie* to a close at last, and they went into rehearsal for *Saint Joan* with Lewis and the author himself co-directing (Lewis also playing de Stogumber) and a cast which, apart from Sybil, included Raymond Massey as La Hire, Ernest Thesiger as the Dauphin and a fourteen-year-old Jack Hawkins as the Page. The sets were by Charles Ricketts who in his time had designed scenery for his friend Oscar Wilde as well as for countless other playwrights; the budget being limited, however (this was to be a joint Sybil Thorndike–Mary Moore presentation at the New), much was achieved by a series of innovatory lighting changes. Rehearsals, according to Russell, proceeded smoothly enough:

Sybil walked on air during that month ... the only thing that depressed her was that none of them could act the play as well as Shaw could. He knew every intonation he wanted and it was always the true, the common-sense thing that he did want ... at the dress-rehearsal, Shaw came on the stage and said, 'Scenery and clothes have ruined my play. Why can't you play it in plain clothes as at rehearsal?' Sybil jumped for joy. She hated scenery and always said she could act better with a towel round her head and her face ordinary.

Nevertheless they kept the costumes, and for G.B.S. Sybil's constant admiration and affection proved a welcome change from his usual treatment at the hands of Mrs Patrick Campbell: 'for a whole month', he wrote smugly to Stella, 'Sybil never let me doubt that she regarded me as far superior to the Holy Trinity as producer ... if only you had faith as much as a grain of mustard seed!' Sybil herself gave an interview just before the first night in which she added:

When Mr Shaw first read the play to us I said to him 'It would be wonderful if you played every part.' His reply was characteristic, 'Oh, dear no. People have quite enough of me as it is. They say I speak in every character, but if I acted every one as well I don't know what would happen.' At rehearsals however he can, and does if necessary. He knows exactly what he wants. That is why I think he is easy to work for in the theatre. He has such beautiful manners that he never hurts. It seems as though he feels it would be an offence against himself to say anything harsh or hard. If he has to, then the criticism is cloaked in such a way that nobody could be offended. He can lay you flat and knock all the conceit out of you without making you feel humiliated. That, in a man with such a tongue, who can flay institutions and people alive as he does, is I think very re-markable. It is part of his charm. At rehearsals he is always very quiet, always courtly, but there is about him the suggestion of a volcano. If anyone set himself against him it would be to discover the force in him, but nobody ever does.

Lewis was marginally less enthusiastic about Shaw's technical expertise in rehearsal, and it's safe to assume that most of the big set-piece crowd scenes were Casson's alone, though G.B.S. undoubtedly was of vast help to Sybil and gave her the idea for saying 'Dear-child-of-God' and 'Be-brave-go-on' in the manner of the cathedral chimes. It was also Shaw who insisted Sybil play with a faint but unspecific North Country accent, to get away from the problems of a 'ladylike' Saint who is in any case not even a saint until the very end of the play. Others in the company were also much impressed by the author, though of Sybil herself Ernest Thesiger waspishly wrote some years afterwards that 'I was glad to note, watching her in subsequent revivals, that repose was not an entire stranger to her.' As for Jack Hawkins, he just recalled Shaw reading the part of the Page in 'a ridiculous falsetto – I thought he was quite mad but never-theless tried to mimic him'.

There is to this day a faintly lingering misapprehension that Sybil Thorndike played her Saint Joan as the first really major performance in a career which became distinguished because of it. In fact, at the time she went into rehearsal with Shaw, he was sixty-seven and she was already forty-two, having been on the stage more than twenty years and being the proud holder of an honorary doctorate from Manchester University. But this was indeed the peak of her career, and situated nearly midway

With Ernest Thesiger as the Dauphin (*centre*) in the cathedral, *Saint Joan*, New Theatre, March 1924: 'Joan was excellent – boyish, brusque, inspired, exalted, mannerless, tactless, and obviously, once she had served her turn, a nuisance to everybody. The part is one which no actress who is leading lady only, and not artist, would look at. But Miss Thorndike is a noble artist, and did nobly.' (James Agate, *Sunday Times*)

through her long life: it was a peak on which she was to remain for nine years with the subsequent revivals of the play (her last stage appearance as Joan was in New Zealand at the beginning of 1933, though she went on doing it on radio into the 1950s) but after it, as her son John has said, there were to be no more of her great leaps forward.

*Saint Joan* opened at the New Theatre on 26 March 1924: the year, suitably for Sybil's politics, of Britain's first Labour government and in the theatre also the year of Coward's *The Vortex*, though of precious little else.

Another of the lingering misapprehensions about *Saint Joan* is that it was an immediate critical success. Certainly it was an immediate public success: Archibald Haddon, the BBC's first and only fully accredited theatre critic, reported on the air that 'public interest was so intense that a queue began to assemble at five o'clock in the morning. More than two thousand applications for first-night tickets had to be refused, and when the curtain rose celebrities were as plentiful in the audience as they used to be at Henry Irving's Lyceum or Herbert Tree's His Majesty's.'

To her own considerable surprise, Sybil told me several years later, she felt no nerves at all: 'Usually I'm paralytic with fear before a first night, but for the only time in my life I didn't feel a thing. The moment those trumpets came up I was all right and we played nearly six months there, packed to the doors every night.'

But critics seemed less confident. Christopher Hollis noted later that:

*Saint Joan* was greeted with that howl with which it has become a tradition of English dramatic criticism to greet Mr Shaw's plays. Men asked whether the great revolutionary had turned fascist. Free thinkers whispered Browning's *Lost Leader* to one another in undertones. Broad-minded Mayfair purred, and some Catholics even went so far as to use language dangerously laudatory of the apologetics with which Mr Shaw had been good enough to provide the church. Even Mr Chesterton, if I remember rightly, enthusiastically explained that the Inquisitor was the true hero of the play.

On a first night programme showing the reputed portrait of Joan from an original sculpture formerly in the church of St Maurice, Orleans, *The Times* critic made his notes:

One of Mr Shaw's finest achievements, despite regrettable lapses into the slang of today, such as Joan's habit of addressing the Dauphin as 'Charlie' ... typical but minor Shavian blemishes rather than gaping wounds ... the Epilogue is an artistic error because it lets the play down, robs it of naïvety and imports an

With Jack Hawkins as the Page and Robert Horton as Dunois on the banks of the Loire, *Saint Joan*, New Theatre, March 1924

G. B. Shaw discussing the making of a phono-film of *Saint Joan* with Sybil Thorndike and Lewis Casson; this meeting was successful and Shaw gave permission for the church scene to be made into a five-minute film, July 1927

incongruity – the frock-coated cleric. . . . Sybil Thorndike plays Joan quite beautifully, rather like a headstrong boy (we do not hint any horrible likeness to a
'principal boy') . . . she has the very face and voice for it, a keen intelligence,
too, without which a great Shaw part would surely become a great infliction. . . .
Mr Thesiger is too farcical as the Dauphin.

Most other critics were equally sure about Sybil and uncertain about
the play. Maugham thought 'Shaw talks too much and too long', and
for the *Daily Telegraph* W. A. Darlington pointed out that of all the half-
dozen Joans he was later to see (including Wendy Hiller, Celia Johnson,
Siobhan McKenna and Joan Plowright) 'none to my mind has given us
the two sides of the part, Joan the peasant and Joan the saint, so completely
as Dame Sybil'. For the *Sunday Times*, Agate expressed grave doubts
about Shaw's characterization ('he is at enormous pains to prove that Joan
was really an Arnold Bennett heroine born five hundred years before her
time') but concluded:

The production was beyond any praise of mine. The scenery, designed by Mr
Charles Ricketts, was neither frankly representational nor uncompromisingly
expressionistic, but a happy blend of the two. The dresses made a kind of music
in the air, and at the end Joan was allowed to stand for a moment in all that
ecstasy of tinsel and blue in which French image-makers enshrine her memory.
As Joan Miss Thorndike had three admirable moments: when she said, 'They
do!', when she listened in the Ambulatory to the pronouncement of desertion
to come, and when she listened to the reading of her recantation. May I beseech
Mr Shaw to allow her to drop the dialect? Whatever the quality of Lorraine
peasant-speech, it cannot have been Lancashire, and there was too much the
smack of Oldham about such sentences as 'Ah call that muck!' and 'Th'art not
King yet, lad; th'art nobbut t'Dauphin.' Apart from these eccentricities, which
were not of the actress's seeking, Joan was excellent – boyish, brusque, inspired,
exalted, mannerless, tactless, and obviously, once she had served her turn, a
nuisance to everybody. The part is one which no actress who is leading lady only,
and not artist, would look at. But Miss Thorndike is a noble artist, and did nobly.

The author himself was in agreement, at least with the end of Agate's
notice. Shortly after the first night Sybil received a copy of his script in-
scribed 'to Saint Sybil Thorndike from Saint Bernard Shaw'. As for
Lewis, when he saw the reviews he told Sybil, 'Well, we're good for six
weeks anyway.'

That first production of *Saint Joan* ran at the New Theatre for 244 performances and for almost every one of them Sybil's mother played the
organ offstage in the Cathedral scene. They then had to make way (while

Miss Sybil Thorndike.

Drawn by George Belcher.

"What's Hecuba to her," and what St. Joan?
Much, for she sees their sorrows as her own.
Ancient or modern, where she walks the stage,
She stamps her art on work of any age;

EURIPIDES she brings to our address,
And makes a classic out of G.B.S.
Oh, may her honoured name endure as long
As the old Sibyls' (though she spells it wrong)!

Punch cartoon, 1924

still playing to capacity) for Matheson Lang who had booked the theatre months earlier, and the Cassons took to the provinces in a tour of the ever-reliable *Lie*. They then got the Regent Theatre, King's Cross, where with virtually the original cast they revived *Saint Joan* and lasted another 321 performances, which meant that between March 1924 and May 1925 they achieved a run of over 500 performances, a record that very few serious plays have ever challenged on their first outing. And in the end, as Archibald Haddon said, the memory was of Sybil:

What a picture she is in her resplendent suit of armour – the fine poise of her body in the cathedral at Rheims – her bright auburn hair falling short at the neck, her radiant face uplifted in celestial rapture, listening to the voices of her saints! How the grand voice moves you when the distracted girl turns on her persecutors of the Inquisition and pours on her judges the vials of her righteous scorn! This is Joan of Arc incarnate. It is a great, an inspired, creation. As a feat of acting it compels enthusiasm. It is a precious jewel in Sybil Thorndike's crown.

Ivor Brown wrote in 1954:

Of all the Joans I have seen, I fancy that Sybil Thorndike came nearest to bridging the gap between the tough and tender Joans and making the best of both the histrionic worlds. Furthermore she had a laughing way in the teeth of the world, whose gaiety is in the text but is often missed in performance.

And, as Sybil herself said, looking back on Joan fifty years later, 'I felt somehow that I never wanted to do anything else, that I'd reached something I could never reach again and I was just so grateful that the audience were there night after night to see me reach it.'

# 'We brought the air back to the earth'

Undeterred by the fact that Joan is one of the longest and most arduous parts written for a woman in twentieth-century theatre, Sybil continued during the play's initial run with her practice of doing special matinées of other work, either for charity or simply to try out a promising new writer; thus during 1924–5, she did Sonia in Ernst Toller's *Man and the Masses*, Rosalind in *As You Like It*, Claire in *The Verge* and Hecuba, Phaedra and Artemis in various Gilbert Murray translations from the Greek. Of these, it was *The Verge* which most impressed her; in 1962 she told Derek Prouse:

That meant a great deal to me, and I can still remember some of Susan Glaspell's dialogue: 'I thought when we were flying, when suddenly we broke into the air, we were going to break into a new life – but no, we've brought the air back to the earth.' That is an expression of the kind of adventurous spirit we need. That play also dealt with the dangers of conformity, something that I've always tried to fight. Once you give an idea a name and you pin it down, you deep-freeze its vitality. You may have made it comfortable to live with, but you've drained it of all meaning; you've lost the chance of making a real leap forward.

That chance of 'a real leap forward' was the one Sybil most cherished, and the determination to take it whenever and wherever possible explains some distinctly curious entries in the catalogue of her performances over the years. But for now, with *Saint Joan* temporarily shelved after its run at the Regent, the Cassons for once had a little money put by; the Shaw play had taken all of their savings and repaid them thrice over, though most of this now went into *The Round Table*, a curious Lennox Robinson disaster at Wyndham's. 'If Sybil Thorndike wants a holiday from *Saint Joan*,' complained the *Express*, 'why doesn't she take one, instead of playing this sort of part?'

The question was unanswerable, and as they had also had a failure at Wyndham's with their presentation of a beloved children's play (*The Rose and The Ring*) the time had clearly come to revive the ever-popular *Lie* yet again. During this run, Lewis and Sybil gave 'a flying open-air matinée' of *Medea* at Christ Church, Oxford, in which 'an old man' was played by an undergraduate of the time, billed on the programme as G. E. Williams and later known as Emlyn:

The setting was the Library façade and pillars; the performance must have been impressive, and perhaps more than that when Miss Thorndike flung open the great first-floor window, distractedly picking up her recumbent daugher Ann and seemed about to throw her at a startled front row of dons. Changing after-wards inside, I admired the professional bustle with which the Cassons packed before the dash for the London train; as they streaked across to Canterbury Gate, the youngest middle-aged couple I had ever seen – 'Lewis darling, the thermos!' – and into a waiting taxi, I stood looking after them, a dog that had been left behind. But next morning I had the luck to run into eighty-nine-year-old Doctor Lock, doyen of the House Canons. 'Miss Thornton,' he quavered, 'was word-perfect, I could not fault her, and I had Professor Gilbert Murray on my knee all through the performance.'

A tour of *Saint Joan* followed, and then, towards the end of 1925, the Cassons elected to take the Empire Theatre in Leicester Square and stage *Henry VIII* there. For it, they assembled a cast considerably more remarkable in retrospect than at the time: Norman V. Norman played the King, Sybil was Queen Katharine and Angela Baddeley was Anne Boleyn. Sybil had three Pages in the court scenes: they were Jack Haw-kins, Carol Reed and Laurence Olivier, who also appeared for his three pounds a week as assorted bishops, lords, officers, guards and scribes. It was Olivier's first West End job, he was eighteen, and he owed it to Sybil's memory of how impressed she had been when his father and her father had taken her to see the young Laurence as Katharina in an All Saints School production of *The Taming of the Shrew*.

This *Henry VIII* was by all accounts more a pageant than a play, but of Sybil's performance Agate wrote that 'in suffering she moves you to the shattering depths of spiritual pity' and it served as a useful reminder to London audiences that she wasn't going to play Joan forever. The Empire, a one-time music hall, seemed a bizarre choice of theatre, though Marie Tempest noted that if anyone could have a Shakespearian success there it was probably Sybil. Olivier remembered his début with pleasure ('my saint and my heroine', he called the Cassons) and stayed with their company into 1926 when they revived both *The Cenci* and *Saint Joan*. Jack Hawkins, too, was still with them, though he was more than a

As Katherine of Aragon in *Henry VIII*, Empire Theatre, Leicester Square, December 1925; Lewis Casson as Griffith

ABOVE As Portia with Lewis Casson as Shylock, Old Vic Company at the Lyric Theatre, Hammersmith, autumn 1927

As Lady Macbeth, Princes Theatre, December 1926, designed by Charles Ricketts. 'Every inch a queen, but she can never stir the blood nor freeze it' – *The Times*

little confused by the Cassons' attitude when in May the General Strike started:

The strike coincided with the opening of the new London season of *Saint Joan*, but because of street demonstrations and the fact that buses and tubes were not running, few people were prepared to go to the theatre. In those days, of course, relatively few people owned cars and many of those who did were reluctant to drive in London. Determined to arrive at rehearsals on time, I set off at six in the morning to walk the eight miles from Wood Green to the Lyceum – but unfortunately arrived five minutes late. I apologised but did not explain why. However, someone mentioned the real reason to the Cassons and from then on they very kindly insisted I stay with them. . . . It was typical of the Cassons' belief in Socialism that while every evening the play was being slaughtered financially by the strike, every morning Lewis would drive TUC leaders to their meetings with Government ministers in his blue Lanchester. In those days, trades union leaders could not afford their own cars. Each evening we would go through the ritual of a performance for the handful of people who formed an audience. Before the curtain went up, either Lewis or the stage manager would go out in front and invite them to come down to the front row of the stalls. 'We shall feel more cosy,' he would explain. But eventually, the situation grew so bad that we were forced to close.

Lewis drove the strike leaders (just as he had once driven for the suffragettes) out of a deep-seated conviction that they and their cause represented a social injustice which had to be righted in their favour. His attitude was always totally and utterly endorsed by Sybil, though the rest of the family were sometimes less enthusiastic: 'Very tactless, is Lewis', said Russell once. 'He never plays up to the government that's in.' Even his son John was somewhat confused by Lewis's ardent Socialism:

When the General Strike caused *Joan* to fold up, Lewis went off to the North of England with his Armstrong Siddeley and a huge label TUC on the windscreen to be a courier-cum-carrier-cum-taxi for any strike officials who wanted themselves or their messages carried from place to place. Before he left he drove me back to the *Worcester*, a week late for the summer term, because there were no trains, and we drove down through the Elephant and Castle and New Cross and Dartford to Greenhithe. This was a 'poor quarter' all the way. Angry looking groups of men stood at street corners and people well-off enough to drive around in motor cars got booed and shouted at. But our TUC label did the trick and we made the journey without getting into trouble. During the hour's run, Lewis tried to explain to me what it was all about and why he was behaving quite differently from all our friends . . . 'these people who are on strike don't want

Leading the procession for Women Peace Pilgrims, Hyde Park, London, June 1926
At home with Mary and Ann, 1925

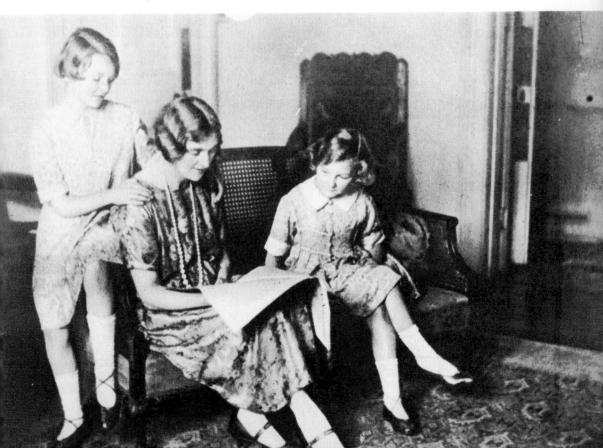

a rebellion or even a riot. They just want a fairer share of the things they are making with their own hands in the factories . . . when you do work on something, you give it value. And if you do the work you ought to have a big share of the value. Nothing has value till work is done on it, and we own what all of us agree as a country that we are allowed to own. These strikers don't want to take things away from others. They feel they might own a slightly fairer share, that's all. They're not bad or vicious. They're frightened and hungry people and their wives and children are frightened and hungry. Just look at their faces as we go by and you'll see what I mean.' And I did look at their faces through his clearer eyes, and I did see what he meant.

But if Lewis was preoccupied with driving for the strike leaders ('his car was called up', said Russell) Sybil was still not going to budge far from the theatre; if she could not act in it because of the Strike, she could at least teach it since she had for some time been giving lessons in Greek tragedy at RADA:

One class I had, it must have been about 1922, was really awful – they were all like a lot of governesses, no power, and I said, 'You're all terrible, no fire, no guts, you've none of you got anything in you except that boy over there, the tall one, what's your name?' And he said, 'It's John Gielgud,' and I said, 'Well, you're the only one.' The rest of them had no voices, and I was furious with the principal because all his pupils were perfect ladies and gentlemen and that's no way to do Greek tragedy. They all looked as though they were training to be Gerald du Maurier.

When the Strike came to an end, Sybil did a special matinée of the uncut *Hamlet* in aid of the Sadler's Wells Fund. Ben Greet directed (much assisted by Lewis) and Russell played Hamlet with his sister as Gertrude and Fay Compton as Ophelia. It was a considerable ordeal for all concerned, not least because Greet was now ailing and Russell still suffering from his war wounds. Sybil however sailed through it all undaunted, having discovered early on the morning of the performance that her Psalm for the Day was the one starting 'And the Lord shall rehearse it'.

The next play the Cassons did for a run was an early Clemence Dane called *Granite*, which was set on a cliff high above Lundy Island and involved Sybil as the passionate Judith Morris and Lewis as a devilish stranger inclined to hurl her successive husbands into the sea. It was not a subtle play, indeed it reminded several onlookers of the dear dead days of the Cassons in Guignol, but it gave them both the chance to pull out all the stops in one of those joint histrionic *tours-de-force* which were to recur throughout their careers like avalanches, leaving spectators out of breath and thoroughly impressed yet not always in favour of the event.

The public remained, as so often, unimpressed with Sybil at her noisiest and *Granite* lasted barely six weeks at the Ambassadors though Mrs Patrick Campbell avowed it was one of her favourite plays as, more mysteriously, did the Indian mystic Tagore. After it closed the Cassons took their four (and some now teenage) children to France where they explored all the Joan country around Rouen and survived Lewis's driving for nearly a month. For the autumn, they planned to tour both *Saint Joan* and *Henry VIII* around England, but it was clearly time Sybil started to work on something new and they decided that she'd better try another Lady Macbeth since there hadn't been one since the Vic nearly a decade ago. Henry Ainley was to be her Macbeth, and the plan was for Lewis again to direct and for Ricketts to design. There was also to be music by Granville Bantock which, said John Casson, contained 'passages of ominous and heavy brass that would have scared the daylights out of Genghis Khan'.

This production was however doomed in more ways than one; Ainley, having survived a ten-hour dress rehearsal, was taken ill early in the run and replaced by Hubert Carter who, though a long-time reliable stalwart of the Casson company, allowed the role to go to his head and, nightly in the duel scene, all but killed Basil Gill as Macduff until Lewis had stage-hands posted out of sight among the scenery to hiss at Carter during the duel that Macbeth was intended by the author to lose it. Business held up well during the school holidays but then fell away sharply, and Sybil's own reviews had been curiously mixed; by rights the part should have been hers above all others, though J. C. Trewin reckoned that 'she fought with it through the years and yet never quite established it as her own' the way she established proprietary claims to Joan, Hecuba and Medea. At the time of this 1926 *Macbeth*, *The Times* thought her technically fault-less and 'every inch the Queen' but added that 'she could never stir the blood nor freeze it', and Agate thought she lacked 'any sense of awe, superstition or poetry'.

Sybil admitted to the family that she had not got Lady Macbeth right yet, and was indeed never again to play her in London though she frequently revived the play at home and abroad up to the middle of the war. But her London failure in 1926 was sadly to set the tone for several years to come. Now that the public had taken her to their hearts as Joan (and it was only to be a matter of half a decade before that perform-ance had so entered the mythology of the nation that Muriel Spark's Jean

Brodie could, in prewar Edinburgh, instruct whole schoolrooms of girls to 'hold up your heads like Sybil Thorndike') they were unwilling to see her do much else. Between the opening of *Saint Joan* in 1924 and her first night as Miss Moffat in Emlyn Williams's *The Corn is Green* in September 1938 Sybil Thorndike made stage appearances in nearly a hundred new plays and revivals at home and abroad (an average of just over half a dozen a year) yet none of them has really found its way into stage history except in the reference section. For more than a decade she was, like it or not, Joan and that was more or less that.

She however was to be deterred no more than Lewis by the vagaries of popular taste or box-office fortune. When *Macbeth* folded at the Princes she went straight into a Russian romance by J. B. Fagan called *The Greater Love* which did a great deal of good for a young actor who, much to Fagan's fury, insisted on rehearsing in a dirty raincoat and was called Charles Laughton, but did not materially improve the careers or reputations of anyone else involved.

Next came an invitation to revive *Saint Joan* for the International Festival to be held in Paris during June 1927. They were to play at the Théâtre des Champs Elysées and to add to the excitement the whole company was to fly across the Channel, an event best described (as so many others in the Casson lives) by Sybil in a letter, this one written to her son John:

Well!! We've *done* it! We've *flown*! All the way from Croydon to Paris in a *huge* aeroplane, and the whole company came with us – except Lyall Swete who has to have a cigarette every five minutes and so couldn't bear to go two and a half hours without one – so silly. Think what he missed! When the engines started and we raced across the field I thought I'd die with excitement and quirks. Did *you* feel like that when you flew? Oh, but you're so much braver than me. I was terrified, and thrilled too, of course. Doesn't the earth look gorgeous from up there? All those lovely fields and the comic little houses. I'd taken lots of seasick pills in case, but they didn't work and I was absolutely pea-green. Halfway over, when I was thinking 'I can't bear this another second' Tom Kealy passed me a message which said, 'Note the cultivation of the land.' I could have killed him! I didn't care about the cultivation of anything! But I wasn't actually sick till we went down. Oh, John, that awful 'swing' feeling as you glide down. I don't know how you stood it. As we got out we saw a huge crowd of French people waving flowers and hats at us. All those nice actors and actresses. I just had time to dash into the Ladies and be very sick – all my breakfast – put on some make-up and then come back and make a speech to them all – in French! But they were all sweet and then Captain Boris and his wife came up and we all hugged each other. You remember his coming to Wood Street in the war with all those gorgeous French chocolates? Well, let's hope they all like the play. We open the day after tomorrow. ...

PPS The French are all darlings.

Darlings they may have been, keen to see *Saint Joan* played in English they were not; with the usual Casson financial luck and acumen the box-office takings did not match up to the considerable cost of airlifting the company, and as usual they had to meet the difference. Then, after a brief summer holiday in Wales, they were back in London wondering what to do next when they were approached by the redoubtable figure of Lilian Baylis, still in charge of the Old Vic where Sybil had last played in 1918 but now in even more economic and technical troubles than usual. The Vic had to close that winter in order to allow the auditorium to be restructured, and the Princes, which had seemed to Baylis a likely place to move her company for the duration, was asking a rental of four hundred pounds a week which she considered altogether too much. She could however get Nigel Playfair's Lyric, Hammersmith, for a mere three hundred and ten pounds but what she couldn't get was an actress to lead the company there since Edith Evans had made it clear that her next appearance should be in the West End rather than west of Kensington.

Predictably, Sybil leapt into the breach and headed the company during their Hammersmith exile, playing Katharina, Portia, Beatrice and then doubling the Chorus and the Princess of France in *Henry V*. Lewis (temporarily freed by Baylis from the burdens of management) for once allowed himself to come to the fore as an actor and played Petruchio, Shylock, Benedick and Henry V, performances which were to live in the memory of those who saw them long after another generation had come to accept him as at best a supporting player.

During this Hammersmith season, Sybil was approached by the film producer Herbert Wilcox who wanted her to play Edith Cavell in *Dawn*. Sybil, though she'd never made a full-length feature film, was immediately drawn to the idea first because the medium of silent movies was something she obviously had to tackle and second because her beloved Bernard Shaw, in his preface to *Saint Joan*, had likened his heroine to Nurse Cavell. Wilcox himself was producing and directing (with Mary Brough and Haddon Mason also in the cast) but before it could be released the film ran into tremendous trouble from people who thought that bygones should be bygones and that *Dawn* would unnecessarily offend German susceptibilities.

The Foreign Secretary, Sir Austen Chamberlain, indeed wrote to Wilcox expressing his 'repugnance to the production' and it was decided not to give the film a certificate for release. Immediately, writers grouped themselves into various camps of opinion. H. L. Mencken, without seeing it, wrote: 'I assume the picture is swinish and abominable but I am unalterably against any effort to stop its showing', a judgement somewhat harsh in view of the film's eminently quiet good taste. Shaw, on the other hand, raced to Sybil's defence: 'You have a most moving and impressive incarnation of that heroine by our greatest tragic actress, whose dignity keeps the whole story on the highest plane. It has been told by a young film poet who has been entirely faithful to his great theme.'

Eventually the row reached the House of Commons, where Chamberlain was on his feet again to denounce the film as 'an outrage on a noble woman's memory to turn for purposes of commercial profit so heroic a story' and eventually Wilcox had to agree to give some of the proceeds to charity before the LCC would licence it on a vote of 56 to 52. *Dawn* was then seen by Richard Watts who reckoned that 'it is an interesting work because it tells a straightforward story (the wartime activities and execution of the nurse Edith Cavell) straightforwardly, is beautifully acted by Sybil Thorndike and, dealing with a theme still full of dynamite, it was thoroughly impartial and honourable in its treatment. But no one could say it was really important as a piece of cinema-making.'

It was however important enough in Sybil's film career. She was to make more than a dozen later silent and talking pictures, but in none of them did she ever again play a major leading role comparable to that of Edith Cavell.

In the end, *Dawn* even made a small profit which is more than could be said for the Cassons' next stage production, an elaborate presentation of *Judith of Israel* (originally meant as a vehicle for Bernhardt but only completed after her death) which lost them a rapid eight thousand pounds at the Strand. Not even a revival of *Everyman* for Ben Greet (with Sybil, Russell and Eileen Thorndike all billed) nor Sybil as Queen Elizabeth to Charles Laughton's Ben Jonson in *The Making of an Immortal* by George Moore could retrieve that kind of loss, so that after a brief season at Wyndham's in *The Stranger in the House* the Cassons set sail for South Africa and a lengthy tour on which they knew they had at least one certain bread-winner. It was of course *Saint Joan*.

As Edith Cavell in Herbert
Wilcox's film *Dawn*, 1928

As Queen Elizabeth in *The
Making of an Immortal*, Arts
Theatre, April 1928

# At Home and (mainly) Abroad

One letter from South Africa sums up the tour, on which Sybil and Lewis together with their daughters and Carleton Hobbs and Walter Hudd gave not only *Saint Joan* but also such earlier Casson vehicles as *The Lie, Jane Clegg, Henry V, Much Ado, Medea* and *Macbeth* (with Lewis now in the title role) as well as a recent Lilian Braithwaite vehicle from the West End, *The Silver Cord*. The letter was written to Russell by Sybil from the Victoria Falls Hotel on All Souls' Day 1928:

We are here at last and Oh! it is the most lovely place. It is impossible for anyone to imagine it ... we left Pretoria at six on Sunday. Huge crowd to see us off ... we woke on Monday at Mafeking and walked about the station and railtrack for an hour. Only seven o'clock. Then we got into Bechuanaland. I can never describe the heat of that day on the train. Parched land, rainless sky, and this scorching baking sun. We got out of the train every time it stopped, and we existed through the day very dirty and continuously passing native villages and natives in every stage of undress, but so beautiful. When sunset came we all sang hymns of joy and watched with eagerness the lovely golden pink of the sun, and the moon coming up at the same time ... next morning we had crossed the border into Rhodesia and saw the Union Jack again as it's all-British Territory. We arrived at Bulawayo at 8.30. Just what I've always imagined. Men in white and sun-helmets ... last night we had an awful lark. We played at Livingstone. Such an experience. Just like a Parish entertainment. The Pianola which is the orchestra had gone wrong, so Mary [Casson] played the piano before the play and between the Acts. Jolly well, too. No music. Making it all up and fitting it together just like proper overtures and entr'actes. We played *The Lie* and before we all swam in the Zambezi, being very careful of crocodiles as there was a show ... the theatre was the Bioscope. It was jolly. The Governor was there and he's treated as the King, so I had to rush and play God Save The King directly I'd finished my curtain calls at the end. ...

Through South Africa the Cassons had travelled, then through Rhodesia and finally back to Cape Town for Christmas. Along the way they also met General Smuts, had what must have been one of the first of the now traditional rows between English actors and local authorities about not playing to segregated audiences, and converted a large number of cinemas into theatres for one night only. This was Sybil's first major foreign tour since her pioneering days in California, and her enjoyment of it (together with an enthusiasm for her work which seemed throughout the thirties to be greater the further she got from London) was to set the tone for many future travels.

Back home again, Lewis found himself in tax troubles and the two of them went straight into a revival of *Major Barbara*, curiously the first and last time Sybil was to play that part, though in the film she did turn up as Mrs Baines. The stage revival (which opened on 5 March 1929 at Wyndham's) had Baliol Holloway as Undershaft, Eric Portman as his son, Lewis as Adolphus Cusins and Michael Redgrave's mother Margaret Scudamore as Lady Brit; it was the third London revival since the play's première in 1906 and lasted barely a month. Despite some generally good reviews, the production (by Lewis and Charles Macdona) suffered from what John Casson called 'Old Vic heartiness'.

His parents then went into another tailor-made but sombre Clemence Dane (*Mariners*, in which the *Granite* relationship was reversed and Sybil dominated Lewis, but still to no avail as it lasted less than a month) and followed it with revivals of *Jane Clegg* and *Medea* (played in a single evening) before ending the year with Sybil as Madame de Beauvais and Lewis as Napoleon in *Madame Plays Nap*, a comedy for which Ivor Brown in the *Saturday Review* did not much care:

Miss Thorndike has decided that the pawnbroker's wife who made rings round Napoleon is a figure of farce. At any rate, she plays it as such, for her performance is a demonstration of energy, of antics, of skippings, of hoppings, of furious frivolity – in short, of what the vulgar would call 'getting away with it'. A critic should always salute efficiency, and on the first night Miss Thorndike did get away with it. Accordingly I tender my salute. But my obeisance is made with reservation. ... Miss Thorndike should not be so seized with the spirit of the festive season as to confuse Madame Bertrand of Paris, 1793, with that group of noble dames whose home is in pantomime. The part, to put it with a more seasonable politeness, is over-played.

The year 1929 had thus not been a good one for either of the Cassons at home; but whereas Lewis knew he could always get work as a director (and was by now beginning to take an interest in the management not only of individual plays but also of his entire profession through what was soon to become known as Equity, of which union he was a founding father) for Sybil the outlook was rather more bleak, not that she would ever have acknowledged it as such. The public, it seemed, would accept her as Joan and for brief seasons of Greek tragedy; beyond that, be it for other Shavian work or modern comedies or Clemence Dane dramas, audiences remained less than wildly impressed and Sybil, despite the constant help and devotion of Lewis, now lacked a firm power base such as the Old Vic or regular West End employment could afford other actresses of her time. She was out on a difficult limb, renowned for playing larger-than-life historical figures at a time when there were no subsidized companies to finance the pageant-like plays in which she specialized, and at the same time both too big vocally and too distinguished for run-of-the-mill commercial theatre employment.

This was a situation in which Sybil (with occasional respite) was to find herself for much of the two decades either side of the war, and one with which she coped simply by playing whatever she was offered whenever and wherever she was offered it. In the whole history of the English theatre it is hard to think of any leading actress who ever turned down so little work. Acting for her was not a matter of playing selected parts and then waiting between times for the next 'right' one to come along: acting was a matter of going down to the theatre every night and playing something.

The year 1930 started for her with Benn Levy's first play *The Devil*, then *Phèdre* with Celia Johnson at the Arts, all in French but like the Levy worth less than a month; then came a bizarre stint at the Everyman, Hampstead, in Georg Kaiser's *The Fire in the Opera House*, an eccentric venture best remembered by Emlyn Williams who, down from Christ Church, had one of his earliest professional engagements in the first week of its run:

I dived into the Tube for the Everyman in Hampstead, worked for twenty minutes – 'You're a dear boy to spare the time' – and dived back. The same procedure was followed for the seven shows: Tube, a scramble into my uniform as 'the Usher', and down to the dark congested wings where Miss Thorndike joined me for our entrance, phosphorescent with friendship. By the time she was launched on her indefatigable part, I was Underground. I never saw anything of the play and had no idea what it was about: all I took in was that, as 'Sylvette', she was in Chinese trousers and a coolie hat. Was she dressed for an opera? 'Turandot'? some time later I asked her. 'I don't remember, dear. Gosh, I must have been nearly fifty then. "Sylvette", I ask you. I must have looked like English mutton dressed as Chinese lamb. Strange little play, I rather loved it. ...'

With Lewis Casson as Adolphus Cusins in *Major Barbara*, Wyndham's Theatre, March 1929

As Emilia with Paul Robeson as Othello and (*on the bed*) Peggy Ashcroft as Desdemona, Savoy Theatre, May 1930

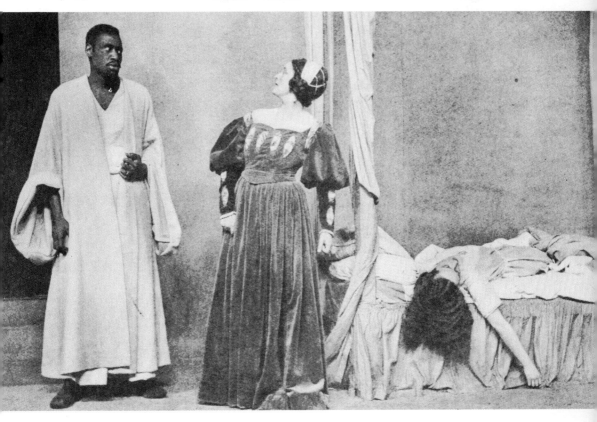

But there was better to come. Williams got into Edgar Wallace's *On the Spot* and Sybil heard that Paul Robeson was coming over to do *Othello*, a production she regarded as a major breakthrough in race relations and one in which she had to be involved. True, Peggy Ashcroft had already been cast as Desdemona, but mercifully she was now old enough for Emilia. Ralph Richardson was also in that cast, playing Roderigo, but a generally uneasy time was had by all. The producer, Ellen van Volkenberg, made Sybil spell her name at the audition and from then on things did not much improve. The production itself was the brainchild of Maurice Browne who had made his money out of *Journey's End* and was now keen to play Iago, and they opened at the Savoy in May 1930. The sets by James Pryde were immensely realistic and therefore very heavy, requiring in Eric Keown's view a demolition squad rather than scene-shifters for the set changes. Whoever they were, they used nightly to drown Desdemona's willow song until Sybil instructed them to wait until it was Emilia's turn to speak, on the grounds that she could outshout any scene change. The sets also required very dim lighting, so dim that Richardson used to carry an electric torch up his sleeve for emergencies. Still the reviews were ecstatic, especially for the Desdemona–Emilia bed-chamber scenes and for Robeson throughout.

Another long regional tour followed *Othello*, and then in April 1931 the last West End revival of Sybil's *Saint Joan* and almost immediately after it, as if the Palace knew the time had now come, the announcement in the Birthday Honours that she was henceforth to be known as Dame Sybil. At the time, she was playing opposite Wolfit at the Embassy in Swiss Cottage in a minor disaster called *Marriage by Purchase* ('Sybil Thorndike Miscast' headlined the *Telegraph*) and Wolfit led her down to the footlights for a highly theatrical moment of celebration. She was the sixth actress in British history to become a Dame (the others being Edith Lyttelton, May Whitty, Genevieve Ward, Ellen Terry and Madge Kendal) and the first to get it on the younger side of her fiftieth birthday. Sybil remained convinced it was all the doing of Bernard Shaw and his friendship with Ramsay MacDonald and the Labour leadership of the day.

The honour did not however distinctly improve her stage fortunes, though she made a couple of films around this time (*To What Red Hell*, which they had to reshoot almost entirely since the coming of sound co-incided with its release, and the first talking version of *Hindle Wakes*) and she also played Madame Duval on the screen in *A Gentleman of Paris* for Michael Balcon.

With Belle Chrystal (*centre*) and
Edmund Gwenn in the film of *Hindle
Wakes*, 1931

1932 Australian tour, Lady Macbeth

By 1932, the time had clearly come for another of her marathon tours, though before that she went briefly back to the Vic to do the Citizen's Wife in *Knight of the Burning Pestle*, again with Ralph Richardson who recalled for Elizabeth Sprigge that:

Dame Sybil was the first great star I had played with. Five minutes before the curtain went up I wondered if I dared pay court and wish her well. I went to the door of her dressing-room, but I was afraid to knock in case she was communing with herself before that big part. Then I heard a buzz of talk inside, and tapped. 'Come in, Ralph dear,' Sybil said. 'Won't you have a bun? There really isn't time for introductions.' She was feeding half-a-dozen schoolgirls buns a few moments before the performance. . . . Sybil sees sermons in stones and good in everything. She even saw good in my Othello which was an incredible piece of observation . . . she can make an actor act. Any actor. I've seen her do it. She could act with a tailor's dummy and bring it to life.

The tour which followed *Knight of the Burning Pestle* was to take in Egypt, Palestine, Australia and New Zealand and it was originally motivated (as had been the first African tour) by Shaw's determination to get *Saint Joan* played as soon as possible in those countries with which he'd already done royalty deals. This time however the Cassons and assorted other actors and children were determined to give unusual value for money: along with *Saint Joan*, from the Playhouse they took Maugham's *The Painted Veil* (which Lewis had originally directed there for Gladys Cooper), from their own earlier repertoires they took *Macbeth*, and they took *Madame Plays Nap*, *Advertising April* and *Granite*. For good measure they also took Shaw's *Captain Brassbound's Conversion* and Ibsen's *Ghosts*.

By now, Sybil had played to every conceivable kind of audience the world over: she'd played in theatres, cinemas, churches, disused Methodist halls, in the open air and indoors, to houses of twenty and houses of two thousand. This, she decided, was the moment to put on paper (for an American magazine called *Theatre Arts*) her thoughts about the nature and duties not of an actress – since these were already so deeply embedded within her character that she could as easily have written at length about breathing – but of an audience:

I suppose the art of the theatre is the only form of art of which the public is an integral part, the only form that is not complete without the spectator. In the fine arts of painting, sculpture or letters, the work is complete without any effort of the outside world. It is very helpful to the artist, no doubt, when good hard cash is paid down and the work is sold; but nothing that the purchaser does or feels or thinks about the particular work can alter it. It is a complete and perfect thing, materialized from the artist's imagination and soul ... the popular art of the theatre, however, stands on quite another footing ... a play is not for all time, it is for the actual moment ... it may be that a particular play is chosen to be played again and again through the ages, but the rite of performance is the important thing, and it is newly created with each perform-ance. ...

I think audiences realize extraordinarily little how much they make or spoil a performance in the theatre, and sometimes I wish – and especially do I wish this when the play is of large vision – that (as in Church one has, or is given, a little manual to show what one's attitude of mind should be, and hints how to behave, that the service may not be unfruitful) members of an audience should be handed a few choice words, setting down that too much eating of chocolate, too much blowing of nose and clearing of throat, too much fidgeting of any sort, will prevent the full enjoyment of the play. And let it also be pointed out that these things and their like are a constant source of irritation to fellow members of the audience and induce in the unfortunate actor a feeling closely akin to murder. A quiet body, with a few beads and chains to jangle (the dreadful days of the bangle are over, we hope) a quiet untrammeled mind and a quiet tongue – these three good things will give an atmosphere in which imagination can work. Shakespeare in his Prologues tells the hearers how to receive the play and conduct themselves.

'Don't forget we've come out for an evening's entertainment, will you?' my friends in the audience will say. No, I don't forget that, and I realize there are differences of approach to various entertainments. I am told that a good dinner, with good wine, is the best way to prepare for the enjoyment of a good play. A good dinner – a choice, spare dinner – maybe, but a large dinner and a full one makes the feeder a hard thing to move, and only the most obvious cast-iron humour will reach him, and only the most obvious sentiment will cause the tears to flow down his cheeks. For the enjoyment of sensitive, subtle humour or sentiment – in order to appreciate the full flavour of Gracie Fields or Edith Evans – I suggest spare feeding, because through these artists and their like you will be filled to overflowing with a food of life which will the better spread to all parts of your body if it is not clogged with meat, poultry, suet and ice-cream. For the healthy and normal-stomached, a not-too-vigorous fasting is an excellent preparation for enjoyment. It whets the appetite for exercise, and the mind and body prepared for exercise are the sort of mind and body the actor hopes to encounter as he leaps or crawls or saunters onto the stage, ready to give forth the superabundant creative energy that he can scarcely restrain. ...

How often do we hear that stupid refrain 'But we have tragedy in real life, why should we have it in the theatre'? Every time this is said to me, with sickening, irritating regularity, it is only by the grace of God and amazing self-control that I am prevented from hurling myself on the speaker. 'You are the servants of the public, you actors, give the public what it wants.' We answer, 'We are not the servants of anyone who does not demand the fullest life. We are the servants of the theatre, of which the public is only a part, and the public doesn't know what it wants till it sees it. Our business is to discover its needs – a very entertaining, intriguing and heartbreaking business. Servant of the public by all means, if by that is meant one who seeks to serve those who do not know what to ask for. The theatre serves those who say "Show us life and that will suffice us".'

That credo delivered, Sybil finished the 1932–3 tour and with it the first half of her life: on tour she'd reached her fiftieth birthday and her last stage performance of *Saint Joan*, and though the travels had been altogether exhausting (the normally unflappable Lewis had indeed reached the verge of a nervous breakdown during his preparations for carting nine full-length shows across to the other side of the globe) it had given them both a rare chance to think about their joint and separate futures.

On their return to London, Lewis went straight into a revival of *Diplomacy* while Sybil got what she called her 'first real modern woman' in John van Druten's *The Distaff Side*. Agate thought her performance here 'glowed like a day in late October' and added 'it is only fair that we should recognise as a property of this actress, and as a possession in her own right, that beauty of mind for which Messrs Euripides and Shaw have too often bagged the credit'. He remained however less impressed by the rest of her work at this time, noting that 'if she is great enough now to be a Dame, she must remain a grande dame', by which he meant could she please avoid plays like *The Double Door* which she did at the Globe immediately after *The Distaff Side* and which involved her in trying to murder a half-sister by locking her up in a safe. Grand Guignol was alive and well and living in Shaftesbury Avenue.

Still, there was better to come. While Lewis went his separate way (throughout the rest of the thirties the Cassons were only very occasionally to work together, this being their one decade of theatrical separation), Sybil did her last London première of a Shaw play (*Village Wooing* at the Little) and then took *The Distaff Side* to New York. She'd not been there for a quarter of a century (since *Smith* in 1910): 'I return', she told an interviewer from the *New York Journal*, 'an aged woman and mature in my reactions. But I find you all amazingly changed, too. Such grand manners! I've really had the most interesting conversations in shops. I

Home again with Ann and Mary

remember when I was last here, people were so abrupt: not rude, exactly, but unpolished. Now you all seem so much more gracious.' Europe, she said, she was considerably more worried about, especially now that both Mussolini and Hitler were in evidence there: 'Goodness knows, I'm all for Nationalism. I myself am a Nationalist. But if Nationalism means being degraded by the force of ruthless leadership, then civilisation itself must be dying in Europe.'

Lewis, between engagements, travelled over to spend Christmas 1934 in New York with her and they took a room at the Gotham Hotel on the floor above Tallulah Bankhead, who used to send them roses and party invitations with equal abandon. Hers was a world Sybil found amazing: 'Quite often, just as I was going off to the theatre to rehearse at ten in the morning, Tallulah would come in and say "I'm off to bed now, darling, shan't stir until the show tonight".'

Edith Evans was also playing on Broadway that season (as the Nurse in *Romeo and Juliet*) and it was Sybil who had the sad task of comforting her when the news came that Edith's husband had died back in England.

Sybil had collected some glowing reviews in the autumn ('she won all our hearts', wrote Brooks Atkinson for the *New York Times*, 'and the simplicity, quiet force and womanly beauty of her drew the audience close around her'), but once *The Distaff Side* closed there was nothing to keep her in America. Back home, she went into a drama called *Grief Goes Over* about which the least said the better and then, in November 1935, played Lady Bucktrout in Robert Morley's first play *Short Story*.

But this was not for Sybil an altogether happy experience ('I'd not want to carry on with this', she told the author as the run came to a fairly rapid end, 'not for all the money in Howard and Wyndham's') though she and Marie Tempest were at the head of a distinguished cast which also included Margaret Rutherford, Rex Harrison and Ursula Jeans. Miss Tempest (who two years later was to become the next actress after Sybil to get the honour of Dame) and she did not often see eye to eye, largely because Miss Tempest used to knit ostentatiously downstage during Dame Sybil's big scene. Finally, and in some desperation, Sybil began playing cards equally ostentatiously during Miss Tempest's big scene, and next night in the wings there was a hissed confrontation: 'Clever little actress, aren't you, dear?' said Miss Tempest. 'No,' replied Sybil sweetly, 'but clever enough to act with you, dear.'

By now Sybil, Lewis and Russell were all so thoroughly established in the theatre (albeit at rather different levels) that legends began to grow

As the Postmistress in Shaw's *Village Wooing*, Little Theatre, June 1934; Arthur Wontner as 'a famous author'

Lady Bucktrout (*far left*) in Robert Morley's *Short Story*, Queen's Theatre, November 1935: (*left to right*) Marie Tempest, A. E. Matthews, Rex Harrison and Una Venning

around them: Russell was the real eccentric of the family, a man known to queue up to see himself and then inform an amazed box-office manager that he'd come to watch 'this fellow Thorndike who they all say is so good'.

Lewis's image was considerably more avuncular: though a passionate and even violent man by nature, he was now directing all the surplus energy which had once been at the call of the suffragettes and the strikers towards the running of Equity, whose second President he was soon to become, and beyond that managing to stay constantly in work as both actor and director, though in both roles his achievements often seemed better appreciated by those inside the acting profession than by mere observers.

As for Sybil, having decided that she and Lewis were bound together forever ('we were held together by the children, you know, when things sometimes got difficult, though we never really thought of breaking up. We fought like cat and dog but never about serious things like the family – we only fought over the theatre and politics, though I suppose they were serious enough too. But think how boring it would have been if we'd always agreed about everything') she persevered with whatever jobs managers cared to throw her way.

'Audiences', she once said, 'are electricity one night and porridge the next', and the same might well have been said for the jobs she was getting in the middle 1930s, though there was rather too much porridge and too little electricity for many tastes. After *Short Story* she played the wife of a Boer farmer in *Farm of Three Echoes* and an old lady terrorized by thugs in an adaptation of a Hugh Walpole chiller. Then came a brisk provincial tour with Lewis and two of the children who were now in the business (Christopher and Ann) on which they did a D. H. Lawrence (*My Son, My Son* which eventually became known as *The Daughter-in-Law*) as well as one-act plays by Shaw and Noël Coward who noted, more in exhaustion than admiration, that 'nobody has ever liked anybody as much as Sybil loves everyone and everything'.

Then came another film (*The Tudor Rose* with Nova Pilbeam as Lady Jane Grey and Sybil cast as the lovable old nurse, the first of a series of cliché-ridden old ladies who were to be her usually unrewarding lot in the cinema, given the generally cautious casting which prevailed in that medium throughout the second half of her life) and then another job with Lewis. This was *Six Men of Dorset*, Miles Malleson's play about the Tolpuddle Martyrs which he and the Cassons took on a lengthy tour totally financed by the TUC in a rare example of union support for the theatre. This Sybil followed with a mindless American domestic comedy (*Yes My Darling Daughter*) and then another Hecuba:

I used to keep in touch with the Greeks whenever possible for good practice. After playing a very dramatic role, the kind only they ever really provided, it's like having a bath, wonderful, you come out all refreshed and clean. When I played Medea, I used to work off all the aggression inside me, and my murderous temper, and when I got home from the theatre all the children said how unusually sweet and gentle I was around the house.

Early in 1938 Sybil went back to Broadway, this time to play Mrs Conway in Priestley's time play: 'There is something big in *Time and the Conways*,' she told an interviewer from the *Herald-Tribune*, 'bigger than the story it appears to tell about one English family. My part is symbolic of the world as it is now – of Europe so torn and troubled and the Empire in disarray. It's about how we all muddle along, clinging desperately to things that have been, just wanting to keep things because we've always had them.'

America did not however take kindly to Priestley's space-time philosophy, and by March Sybil was back at the Old Vic rehearsing for what many would consider her one major and original performance of the thirties thus far, Volumnia to the first Olivier Coriolanus. Lewis was directing, and by general critical and public reckoning the result was the greatest Vic success of Olivier's prewar years:

I think [said Sybil] Lewis did make Larry get rid of some of his little tricks on stage and be more orthodox. Not that he was very tricky as Coriolanus. But if there were tricks, Lewis hated them. He liked straightforward honest-to-God playing. He and Larry got on terribly well. Of course they fought – naturally, because they were both so violent. But they only argued like fun because Lewis loved a good argument. On one occasion Lewis said, 'You've got to do this speech all in one breath.' And Larry said, 'I bet *you* couldn't.' So Lewis did it all in one breath and said, 'Now you do the same.' And of course Larry could do it. After that they used to have breathing contests and Larry always won. He could do the General Confession, 'Almighty and Most Merciful Father' from the morning prayer twice through in one breath. Lewis could only do it one and a half times.

Reviews for this *Coriolanus* were mixed: 'Magnetic Olivier Gabbles', headlined the *Daily Herald* critic, though Ivor Brown, Alan Dent and J. C. Trewin were all enthusiasts. The latter thought Sybil 'too cosily domestic' in the first half of the play, however, and Agate was equally uncertain of her:

If I am in two minds about Sybil's Volumnia it is because she herself is in two minds about the part. Was Shakespeare? In the first half Sybil beams and fusses like a seaside landlady getting on terms with her lodgers. Charles Young, the actor, says of Mrs Siddons's Volumnia that, when her son returned to Rome, 'she towered above all around her, and almost reeled across the stage; her very soul as it were dilating and rioting in its exultation until her action lost all grace, and yet became so true to nature, so picturesque and so descriptive, that pit and gallery sprang to their feet, electrified by the transcendent execution of the conception'. Sybil attempts nothing of this and, when her son returns, receives him with a look of tenderness which, however, is the bridge between her earlier humour and the Hecuba tap now turned on and kept running to the end.

During the *Coriolanus* run, weekends were spent either at Swan Court where Sybil and Lewis already had the flat that was to last them the rest of their lives, or else at Bron-y-garth, the Welsh cottage that Lewis's nephew Hugh Casson had helped them to rebuild. There was still time, however, for Sybil to involve herself in a world above and beyond that of the theatre. It was John Casson who, in a radio tribute after his mother's death, explained:

During the 1930s Sybil discovered that a good actress is also a good public speaker, and she became much in demand to speak for any cause in which her broad humanity could be used to gain followers. She spoke at settlements in the East End of London; she spoke to miners' political gatherings in Wales and sang 'The Red Flag' with them; she sat on platforms with distinguished men and women of India and pleaded for their country's independence; and above all, she spoke for the cause of Pacifism. She was always a great joiner: she was forever joining clubs, associations and institutions for the promotion of every cause from the saving of the lives of multi-coloured guinea pigs in Persia to petitioning the Archbishop of Canterbury to lead a delegation to talk to Hitler. Some of her memberships led her into hot water, but oddly enough not many: she was quite superb at explaining how there was no inconsistency between being a subscriber to the *Daily Worker* ('because the editor is such a pet') and being one of the governors of an exceedingly posh girls' boarding school ('after all, the headmistress is almost a socialist – she said so herself') ... hers was not only a greatness of professional skill, which she shared with many others, but also a greatness of heart which compelled her to put herself and her comforts at the bottom of any list.

After Volumnia there was to be one more prewar performance, and this in the most commercially successful run Sybil had enjoyed since *Saint*

Volumnia to Laurence Olivier's
Coriolanus, Old Vic, April 1938

Miss Moffat in *The Corn is Green* by
Emlyn Williams (*standing*), Duchess
Theatre, September 1938

*Joan*. The play was *The Corn is Green*, written by a thirty-two-year-old Emlyn Williams about his own Welsh schooldays, with Sybil playing the part of Miss Moffat, the crusading English schoolmistress who works to get a local pit-boy into Oxford and who was closely based on Williams's own beloved teacher Miss Cooke, so closely in fact that the two women met during rehearsals and pored over his old schoolbooks.

The description of Miss Moffat in the play ('a healthy Englishwoman with an honest face, clear beautiful eyes, a humorous mouth, a direct friendly manner, and unbounded vitality which is prevented from tiring the spectator by its capacity for sudden silences and for listening. Her most prominent characteristic is her complete unsentimentality') was a perfect fit for Sybil and Agate detected 'genius' here. Reviews for the play and for the two central performances (Williams himself was playing the boy, having first thought that Marius Goring might be more suitable) were ecstatic enough to guarantee them a run of nearly two years, briefly interrupted in September 1939 by the declaration of war, first at the Duchess and then at the Piccadilly.

# To the Valleys and Back to the Vic

In the last few months before the war, Lewis had directed the short-lived Ivor Novello *Henry V* at Drury Lane and then gone back to the Vic to become a joint director for their overseas tour in 1939; Sybil had stayed firmly and well placed at the Duchess, save only for a couple of weeks when a burst appendix forced her to leave the cast and Athene Seyler briefly took over as Miss Moffat. By September 1939, Sybil was back in the cast and after a three-week blackout at the time of the declaration she and the company carried on playing *The Corn is Green* through the Spring of 1940. Lewis was now playing Alonzo to Gielgud's Prospero at the Vic, and one night in May the news came that their son John Casson was missing, believed killed in action. Writing in *Plays & Players* thirty years later, John Gielgud recalled:

We were playing *The Tempest* at the Old Vic – 1940 – the black time of the fall of France. Lewis had been Gloucester in *King Lear* and now he was Alonso, the king, whose son Ferdinand he thought to be drowned. One night the word quickly went round the dressing-rooms that John Casson, Lewis's eldest son, was missing. Every line in the Alonso scenes seemed to refer directly to the agonising situation. We dared not meet each other's eyes or his. But Lewis never faltered, went on acting just as usual, betrayed no flicker of emotion – a little brusquer perhaps than usual, but strong and unshakeable as always. Then, some days later, we heard to our intense relief that John was not dead but had been taken prisoner.

Once they were over the anxiety of those weeks, Sybil and Lewis plunged themselves into war work for CEMA, the forerunner of the Arts Council and itself dedicated in the summer of 1940 to encouraging performances of music and drama in churches, schools and halls throughout the country. Lewis had persuaded Guthrie, who had now inherited from Lilian Baylis the running of the Vic, that since the theatre in the Waterloo Road was temporarily dark the Cassons should lead a Vic company on tour through Wales. Guthrie himself was in overall charge, but Lewis it was who decided they should do *Macbeth*:

'Why take a tragedy to the miners?' asked officials at CEMA; 'Because,' replied Lewis, 'I know the Welsh people, I am Welsh and they like a tragedy.' Rehearsals were held in London for a while and then, as the bombing got worse, Guthrie ordered them to head straight for Wales and do the last runthroughs there: 'Leave Paddington at noon', were his instructions, 'if Paddington is still there at noon.'

Lewis had taken the precaution of inviting Lionel Hale to write a 'plain clothes prologue' to *Macbeth* in which he and Sybil pointed out the play's relevance ('You needn't always think of dictators in terms of concentration camps and tanks and aeroplanes. Men don't change in a thousand years. What Macbeth wanted, what all such people want, is power. This is a play about a tyrant, a dictator') and gave an indication of the excitement of its plot for those who'd never come across it before. Sybil doubled Lady Macbeth and the First Witch, and was at her best and happiest in the impromptu surroundings of a fit-up tour:

We've never played to such audiences [she told John later]; none of them moved a muscle while we were playing, but at the end they went wild and lifted the roof with their clapping. This is the theatre we like best – getting right in amongst people. Afterwards they all came round to talk to us. How I love those lilting Welsh voices and what darlings they are!

Ivor Brown added:

To most of their audiences *Macbeth* was an unknown and intensely exciting play. They had not come like a pack of jaded first-nighters and critics who are Shakespeare-sodden and Bard-weary . . . they had come to see what happened and they were spellbound.

They did thirty-seven Welsh one-night stands in ten weeks and then returned to London where the Casson and Guthrie companies were merged for the start of the first Old Vic wartime season at the New Theatre. This they opened in July 1941 with *King John*. Ernest Milton was in the title role and Sybil was Constance at the head of a company which also included Lewis and Ann Casson, Sonia Dresdel, Renee Asherson, Esme Church and Abraham Sofaer. As might be expected, wrote Audrey Williamson:

Sybil Thorndike did not let the possible touch of humour escape her, and she lashed out about her with a vitriolic scorn. But this actress, with Greek tragedy in her bones, knows how to be regal too and in her distraction there sounded that note of deep and heartshaking grief our stage rarely hears nowadays ... in this suggestion of distraught passion Sybil Thorndike was particularly successful.

Then, and also at the New Theatre, came Sybil's last London *Medea*. 'It is', wrote Ivor Brown in the *Observer*, 'a tremendous role, containing both the woman wrong and the woman wronging. In the first aspect Dame Sybil has the russet majesty of a tremendous oak through which the winds of tragedy are sighing; in the second she blazes into vengeance like a forest fire.'

After that success she returned to Wales, taking *Medea* ('it kindles a fire', echoed one miner to Sybil's huge delight) and *Candida* around the mining villages in the north where again she felt more at home than at almost any other time of her long life. Sybil's faults, if such there were, mattered little here: the miners were not looking for the kind of sexual magnetism she had always lacked on stage, nor did they object (as London often did) to her hearty and sometimes heavy-handed tendency to play up rather than play down a role. Subtlety came to her acting only later, but to these wartime audiences she was precisely what great theatre was all about: blazing, fearless, noisy and larger than life, Sybil Thorndike barnstormed her way through the valleys leaving in her wake a trail of audiences who knew that whatever they'd seen it was Acting.

Of all the actors I have seen [wrote Guthrie some years later] the two who in my opinion best combine protean skill with star quality are Laurence Olivier and Sybil Thorndike. Both are more than equal to the long haul and are able, when required, to assume immense nobility, majesty and grandeur. Both excel in the expression of powerful passion. Both can be hilariously funny. Both take almost too much pleasure in the farouche and grotesque, and an endearing, almost childlike delight in looking, sounding and behaving as unlike their 'real selves' as possible. If only more people had the spiritual freedom, the energy and technical skill to find this sort of release, in escaping their everyday self, there would be many fewer unhappy nuisances plaguing themselves and everyone around them.

Now on the verge of her sixtieth birthday, Sybil was still in her prime and indeed her element. True, *Candida* did badly around the valleys (despite the Vic management's belief that it would go over better with the miners than the Greeks) but the state-subsidized CEMA could afford to keep the Casson company going for a while, and it seemed at last that they'd found on this wartime tour a policy and a house style and an odd kind of travelling constancy which was what they'd unconsciously been working towards through all their earlier tours and London seasons. But Sybil still vehemently denied that a permanent company was what she really wanted ('I simply couldn't have a policy: I only want to be lots of different people: isn't that what acting's for?') and by the end of 1942 the Welsh touring, which had also by now featured a new Laurence Housman, *Jacob's Ladder*, as well as the three earlier productions, was over for good.

Staying at the Welsh cottage for a while, Sybil and Russell went to work on a play of his called *The House of Jeffreys* which by December they decided they could open in at the Embassy in Swiss Cottage. It was, given Russell's penchant for the macabre, an account of one of the cannibalistic descendants of the famous hanging judge and Sybil played her complete with a gammy leg. Agate cared not a jot for the proceedings:

La Thorndike made her rentrée tonight in her brother's preposterous play ... after spending thirty years arranging not to be devoured by cannibals, she took to adopting their diet – to wit, devouring a sister missionary. How had she herself evaded the spit? By falling on her portable harmonium and blasting the poor savages with ecstasy. How did she come to find herself at the heart of African darkness? A descendant of the Judge, she had thought to rid herself of the taint in her blood by the old dodge of converting the heathen. Unfortunately the heathen had the opposite idea and converted her ... to watch our old friend throw the mantle of Hecuba, Medea, Phaedra, Queen Katharine, Lady Macbeth and St Joan over a witch-doctored 'rump-fed ronyon' seemed as incredible as to gaze upon Madge Kendal sitting down to a meal of long pig ... though the skill and tact of Sybil's performance are to be gathered from the fact that we did not laugh at her once, not even when she came back from the wine cellar with a bottle of Amontillado with which to wash down Roberta.

'Just like the old Guignol days', said Sybil gleefully, and went straight into an epic wartime Basil Dean 'anthology in praise of Britain' staged on and around the steps of St Paul's and involving a cast of literally hundreds, led by Leslie Howard, Henry Ainley, Sybil and Edith Evans. A week later they re-staged the whole marathon amid the newly-bombed ruins of Coventry Cathedral and then Sybil was off to Ireland (where her son Christopher now lived and where he has acted ever since) at the invitation of Hilton Edwards and Micheàl MacLiammòir. At that time their Gate company was giving annual seasons at the Gaiety in Dublin and Sybil was wanted for Mrs Alving in *Ghosts*, Lady Cicely in *Captain Brassbound's Conversion* and Mrs Hardcastle in *She Stoops to Conquer*, all

As the White Queen (*left*) in *Alice in Wonderland*, Scala Theatre, December 1943.
Zena Dare was the Red Queen and Roma Beaumont was Alice

played within a six-week season. Of her at this time, MacLiammòir wrote:

Essentially English she is yet nationless, essentially of her time she is timeless, a classic creature, golden and brave as a lioness, with a face to reflect every mood of human experience and a voice poured into her throat by the wind of heaven. 'Oh, but it took such a lot of work!' she cried when I said something about it. 'Lewis was often in despair about me.'

No one could describe Sybil Thorndike: you might as well try to describe the Parthenon. She, like it, radiates a sense of power, of sanity and poise, a kind of golden reassurance ... essential truth is the secret of her acting.

Back then to England, to try out a play called *Queen B* by Guthrie's wife Judith Bretherton. Well received in Bristol and Liverpool, it was not somehow considered feasible for wartime London and so instead Sybil went to do *She Stoops to Conquer* for the Vic in Bristol and then into Enid Bagnold's first play *Lottie Dundass* as the murderous Lottie's home-county mother. This carried her through until Christmas, when it was time to play the White Queen (with Zena Dare as the Red one) at the Scala in a Clemence Dane adaptation of the *Alice* books. A month later still, having done another Greek matinée for her beloved Professor Gilbert Murray, she was off to the Orkneys and Shetlands to read poems. Indefatigable certainly, and brave as MacLiammòir had said, but Sybil herself would have been the first to admit that her work at this time was becoming increasingly fragmented.

It was therefore with a sense of considerable relief that she noticed Richardson and Olivier coming back from the war to set up their famous 1944 partnership with John Burrell for the Vic company at the New, and from August of that year until April 1946 she was to remain a permanent member of the company which was by general public and critical consent the greatest achievement of the British theatre in the 1940s.

They started with *Peer Gynt* in which (under Guthrie's direction) Sybil played Aase with Ralph Richardson as Peer, Olivier as the Button Moulder, and Joyce Redman, Margaret Leighton and Nicholas Hannen also in the cast:

We were [recalled Guthrie] to play at the New but while we rehearsed the Opera Company was installed there with so much scenery that we had to rehearse elsewhere. We were lent rooms in the National Gallery whence the rightful occupants, the masterpieces, had been evacuated to secret caves to protect them from bombs. The doodlebug raids were in progress and if, as frequently occurred,

Old Vic Company, New Theatre, August 1944: Aase to Ralph Richardson's Peer Gynt

one seemed to be headed straight for the National Gallery the rehearsal would stop while we all lay down on the floor.

Despite those problems Guthrie's production got the management of his Vic successors off to a flying start:

The character of Peer [wrote Audrey Williamson] demands exceptional virtuosity in the actor: Richardson bounded through the fjords and over the lower mountain slopes of the part with ease; only the ice-clad poetic peaks escaped his ravishing stride. On a level with this performance was Sybil Thorndike's Aase; a peasant whose spirit seemed lined, seared and toughened by adversity just as her face was lined, seared and toughened by the sharp winds of the north. There was a lashing, corded loyalty about this performance, and when the overworn fibre frayed, the old woman's stillness and distress were deeply moving.

Agate took a faintly more jaded view ('Ralph Richardson was excellent and everybody else died or got married or went mad more than competently') but Trewin reckoned that this was 'Sybil's meridian' and that 'Aase's dying voice would have melted marble'.

Within a month at the New she was (in repertory) also playing Catherine Petkoff to Olivier's Sergius in *Arms and the Man*; then came Queen Margaret to his *Richard III*, the Nurse in *Uncle Vanya*, Mistress Quickly in the two parts of *Henry IV* and the Justice's Lady in *The Critic*. Add to that Jocasta to Olivier's Oedipus and you have twenty of the best months of her working life, all spent at the New or on the ENSA tours which took the Vic company through Belgium, Germany and on to the Comédie Française itself. Reviews for the rest of her work, though, were generally respectful rather than ecstatic: 'gnarled and luminous like a painting by Rembrandt' they called her in *Vanya*; 'abundantly alive' in *Henry IV* and 'impressive' as Jocasta, hampered though she undoubtedly was by a heavily jewelled mauve costume. Opinions here too were divided:

This actress [wrote Audrey Williamson] is a great tragedian in Greek drama because she has the courage which these plays need from the actor – the courage to let out the emotional stops. According to the debased standards of West End acting this is not 'done' and it makes some people uncomfortable. But there is only need for discomfort if the feeling let loose is not genuine. The grief that wells up in Sybil Thorndike at such moments is real, not simulated, grief and her Jocasta – small though the part is beside the towering figure of Oedipus – gave us full measure of it.

Old Vic Company, New
Theatre, November 1944:
Queen Margaret in *Richard III*
(Olivier seated left)

Old Vic Company, New
Theatre, November 1945:
Jocasta to Olivier's Oedipus

Sybil's performance was however also viewed by an eighteen-year-old Kenneth Tynan who noted:

I found it jarring. The prima donna tragedienne (an oracular Sybil) with plump arms and a bellowing contralto, given to sudden hawk-like sweeps up and down the stage, she played with that traditional blazing intensity which, so far from illuminating the personality, strangles it into a sort of red-hot anonymity. She treated every line as if it were the crucial line of the play: it was all so ponderously weighted that when the big hurdles approached, the horse couldn't jump.

During the first Christmas of her stint at the New, Sybil would spend the mornings hurrying across to the Palace Theatre for special children's performances of *Alice*; then in the afternoons Margaret Rutherford would take over the White Queen and Sybil would be back in the grown-up classics at the New.

The end of the war came while the Vic company were on tour in Manchester and Lewis and Ann were playing for CEMA in Cheltenham; soon John Casson returned from his wartime imprisonment and gradually the family regrouped before it was time for Sybil to go off to Germany where the Vic company were to tour for ENSA. There they were shown the full horrors of what had happened, and even played a special matinée for the survivors of Belsen; on then to Paris where Sybil found more cheerful news awaiting her. The newly elected Labour government of 1945 had decided that a knighthood for Lewis was to be on their first Honours list. While they were still in Paris he himself brought over there a tour of *Saint Joan* on which their daughter Ann Casson was now playing the title role and Sybil, by dashing across Paris after her own performance, was able to see and enthuse over the closing moments of her daughter's.

# The Tennent years

Soon it was back to London and the Vic, but when the 1945–6 season came to an end Sybil declined to go to New York whither the rest of the company was bound with *Vanya*, *Henry IV*, *Oedipus* and *The Critic*. Instead, she had decided to rejoin Lewis at the King's Theatre, Hammersmith, where Basil C. Langton had a season in which he was offering Ann Casson Electra to her mother's Clytemnestra, and then both senior Cassons the leading roles in a John Huston play about Woodrow Wilson (*Time to Come*).

But this was not an especially happy or distinguished repertory experience, its shortcomings perhaps unfairly highlighted by the fact that Sybil had so recently come from the New and that Lewis was now finding younger players either unwilling or unable to cope with the heightened demands of Gilbert Murray's Greek adaptations. The same could also have been said of younger audiences, and the Wilson play was not a money-spinner either (Agate was his usual schizoid self, congratulating Lewis backstage and then attacking him in print) and so early in 1947 Sybil went back to the West End, albeit in an equally uninspiring Clemence Dane piece entitled *Call Home the Heart*.

During this run, however, J. B. Priestley appeared one night in Sybil's dressing-room at the St James's with his script of *The Linden Tree*, telling her that although there was nothing in it for her he'd much like Lewis for the Professor. Sybil read it, agreed that Lewis had to do it, and added that she'd be willing to play the apparently unrewarding role of Mrs Linden. Michael MacOwan was to direct for the London Mask Theatre company, and it was he who realized the importance of this role to Sybil despite the fact that Mrs Linden was a character fighting as hard as she could against the inroads of a postwar egalitarian world in which Sybil privately profoundly believed and which she welcomed avidly.

In rehearsal, MacOwan told Elizabeth Sprigge:

It was safe to feed Sybil anything, knowing that everything would be absorbed. 'Let me do it. Let me try it' she would say, the moment I suggested anything. Producing her was rather like a lighting rehearsal. 'Bring up No. 3 full. Now take it down to a half. Up a third. Now set.' The only thing I had to do was stop her making faces . . . and although I think that Sybil's performance as Mrs Linden led to a new quietude in some later parts, it also linked up with her Jane Clegg of so many years earlier, which she also played with such impressive reserve.

This was the last time on stage in London that Sybil was to play a subordinate role to Lewis: though never content to be cast as 'Mr Siddons' (a gentleman about whom Lewis often threatened to write a book) he was already over seventy and Robert Linden was to be his last really important stage creation in the West End. Priestley's play ran for more than four hundred performances at the Duchess, and for Sybil this was the start of what Darlington later called 'her astonishing gallery of portraits of contemporary ladies, all subtly varied and minutely observed', and for many onlookers of the time the miracle was that she could breathe so much life into a woman who believed that 'all comfort, content and delight' had shrivelled up in the world.

During this long run, Sybil found the daytime free for two films (Mrs Squeers in Cavalcanti's *Nicholas Nickelby* and Mrs Mouncey in Negulesco's *Britannia Mews* – 'like playing charades again') and as soon as *The Linden Tree* was off she went into rehearsals for St John Hankin's *The Return of the Prodigal* which Peter Glenville was directing with John Gielgud in the lead. 'Not as good as when we did it in 1913 at the Gaiety in Manchester,' was Sybil's verdict, 'too smart, too overdressed this time.' Most of the critics agreed: for the *Evening Standard* Beverly Baxter called it 'the best dressed and best acted bad play in town' and two other critics added that Gielgud in a fair wig and knickerbockers reminded them irresistibly of Danny Kaye.

Sybil rose above all that, went straight into Margery Sharp's *The Foolish Gentlewoman* and then, in the autumn of 1949, began a long and profitable association with H. M. Tennent, the commercial London production company whose managing director Hugh Beaumont had assessed, shrewdly and as usual a flicker in advance of public taste, that Sybil was reaching an age where she could come down from the classical heights and be eased into a succession of comparatively undemanding Shaftesbury Avenue vehicles in which a loving and also ageing public could be soothed by her just as effectively as once they had been shaken and stirred.

With Lewis Casson as Professor Linden in Priestley's *The Linden Tree*, Duchess
Theatre, August 1947

As Mrs Mouncey with Maureen O'Hara in Negulesco's film *Britannia Mews* (1948)

The first of these vehicles was John Perry's *Treasure Hunt*, a comedy which also involved Lewis and Marie Löhr under Gielgud's direction, and through which Sybil alternately wandered and rampaged as the eccentric Aunt Anna Rose whose hat had a seagull perched on the brim. Mindless, pleasant, escapist entertainment and Sybil loved it ('the comedy performance of the year', said *Theatre World*) though Lewis seems to have been more withdrawn, aware perhaps that old age meant having to accept plays which twenty years earlier he'd have turned down flat.

By the time of the 1950 Edinburgh Festival, John Casson was a director of the Glasgow Citizens' and his parents joined the company for him to direct them in a Festival offering of *Douglas*, John Home's eighteenth-century melodrama about which Trewin was ecstatic:

Dame Sybil Thorndike stood there, contriving in poised sculptural dignity to suggest that she had been framed in the heroic mould ... we are often told of the grand manner. Here it was without excessive striving or forced passion. Dame Sybil, speaking and acting as if *Douglas* were new, governed the stage in attitudes beside which a picture of Siddons waned to a hardboard cut-out.

London managements failed to move *Douglas* south, however, and when they played a final week in Glasgow to disappointing houses Lewis noted sharply to his son that:

People nowadays don't want the theatre for large-scale feeling and imagination. They'd rather go to the ballet and opera for it. They know that it's unreal there and so aren't afraid of it. Now we see straight acting realistically on film and television, and so people expect – and actors are trained to give – plain naturalistic realism on the stage. The trouble is that actors aren't trained to act any more and the naturalistic realism is too damned plain. In fact it's bloody dull.

Returning to London, the Cassons entered into negotiations with Charles B. Cochran for Sybil to play her long-desired Queen Elizabeth I in a Clemence Dane history called *The Lion and the Unicorn* in which Lewis was to be Lord Burleigh. Sadly, however, Cochran died suddenly before the production was under way, and no other management was keen to take it over even in this Festival of Britain year, though some time later on recital tours of Australia and New Zealand the Cassons would often perform excerpts from it.

Instead, during that Festival summer, Tennents put Sybil into *Waters of the Moon*, N. C. Hunter's first great success and one which also starred Edith Evans, Wendy Hiller and Kathleen Harrison under Frith Banbury's

Aunt Anna Rose in *Treasure Hunt*, Apollo Theatre, September 1949

direction. This was to become a gold-plated, copper-bottomed Haymarket triumph (835 performances, no less) and it was the one which gave rise to, and doubtless partially financed, the all-star Tennent revivalist policy of the years to come.

'Chekhovian', several critics called Hunter's mixed assortment of guests snowbound in a remote Dartmoor hotel, while for many first-nighters the real fascination lay in seeing the two great Dames on stage together with Edith Evans undoubtedly in the better part: 'at her scintillating best', said *Theatre World*, 'while over against her fascinating volubility was Sybil Thorndike's frosty dignity and disapproval as Mrs Whyte'.

All things considered, they got on remarkably well together though later in the run Frith Banbury had on Dame Edith's advice to reprimand Dame Sybil for overacting at one matinée: 'Yes,' replied Sybil, 'I was rather naughty on Saturday afternoon, but I had two grandchildren in front and I was determined that they should know exactly what the play was about. Consequently much underlining. . . . However I've pulled myself together now and if you come again I think you'll find all is in order.'

This was the only occasion on which Dame Edith and Dame Sybil ever did a prolonged run together, and while Dame Edith cascaded from a great height ('like Royalty opening a bazaar', said Tynan) Dame Sybil contented herself by playing Schumann on the stage and, when the grandchildren weren't in front, capturing the few good scenes she did have almost by stealth. The critics remained uneasy about Hunter as a dramatist, never sure whether he was an imitation Chekhov or a pastiche thereof, and many quoted his famous line 'it is not kind to make us dream of the waters of the moon' as a kind of epitaph.

Yet the play ran and ran, and the Dames survived each other. Twenty years later I asked Dame Edith what she remembered of it all: 'Sybil I always envied for having so many relatives. She had the dressing room above mine, and all I ever seemed to hear was the tramp of children's feet.' Legend has it that when the play had been running successfully for a year, the Tennent management announced to Edith that she'd be getting a whole new wardrobe from Balmain. 'Good,' said Edith, 'but you'd better do something for Sybil, too. What about a new cardigan?'

During that Haymarket run, on 13 June 1951, Sybil read the Poet Laureate's ode aloud while the Queen Mother laid the foundation stone of the National Theatre on the South Bank, by no means that stone's first or last resting-place. When, a quarter of a century later almost to

Family gathering,
Theatre Royal,
Haymarket, 1951: (*left to right*) Russell, Eileen and
Sybil Thorndike with
Lewis Casson

The meeting of the
Dames: Edith Evans as
Helen Lancaster and
Sybil Thorndike as Mrs
Whyte in N. C.
Hunter's *Waters of the Moon*, Theatre Royal,
Haymarket, April 1951

the week, the building eventually opened its doors Sybil was three months away from her death, though only a matter of days before that opening she had been in the audience when the National company had bade its farewell to the Vic and to the ghost of her friend Lilian Baylis.

Throughout her long stage runs in the early 1950s, Sybil took to filming guest-star roles (such as Mrs Gill in Hitchcock's *Stage Fright*, Miss Bosanquet in Wilcox's *The Lady with the Lamp* and Queen Victoria in Milestone's *Melba*) with increasing regularity though her heart was still not in them. In the theatre, the Albery management were now trying to wrest her from Tennent's clutches and put her into Graham Greene's *The Living Room*; but Tennent's counter-offered another N. C. Hunter, one moreover with a role for Lewis whom she was increasingly reluctant to let out of her sight at his advancing age, and as so often it was Beaumont at Tennent's who won the bidding.

The new Hunter was *A Day by the Sea* (also chosen by John Gielgud in preference to a new John Whiting, *Marching Song*) and under Gielgud's own direction and with him and the Cassons was a company which also included Ralph Richardson, Irene Worth and Megs Jenkins. The setting this time was Dorset rather than Devon, but again the quiet tempo and periods of long inactivity brought out the critical comparisons with Chekhov, ones in which Hunter was bound to fare badly. For the *Observer*, Tynan was hugely unenthusiastic: he disliked what he called 'Sybil's almighty cooing' and he reckoned that the play itself was 'an evening of unexampled triviality ... like watching a flock of eagles and macaws of magnificent plumage jammed for two hours in a suburban birdcage'.

Despite (or because?) of that, *A Day by the Sea* did nearly four hundred performances at the Haymarket after an uneasy provincial tour at the start of which Gielgud was involved in a (for the middle 1950s) fairly sensational court appearance. Accordingly there was then some doubt about how an audience would react to Gielgud's first appearance in the play. 'I needn't have worried,' Lewis later told his son, 'Sybil went on stage first and fixed the audience with one of her looks, as though she were saying "I don't think it matters; do any of you?" and daring anyone to think otherwise. Nobody dared.'

During the run of *A Day by the Sea* it was decided, in the curiously arbitrary way such things are often decided, that Sybil had reached her golden jubilee on the stage. The date chosen was 31 May 1954 and she was to share her special gala matinée with the golden jubilee of the found-

(*front*) Patricia Laurence, Irene Worth, Sybil Thorndike, Peter Murphy, Megs Jenkins; (*back*) Frederick Piper, Ralph Richardson and John Gielgud in N. C. Hunter's *A Day by the Sea*, Theatre Royal, Haymarket, November 1953

Queen Victoria in Lewis Milestone's film *Melba*, 1953

ing of RADA and the hundredth anniversary of the birth of Herbert Beer-bohm Tree.

Accordingly, Sir Alan Herbert composed a special if not immensely distinguished Ode for Edith Evans to speak in the presence of the Queen Mother:

'Coincidence!' we cry, when who can tell
If harsh Necessity was there as well.
Just fifty years ago, a glorious age,
A girl called Sybil pranced upon the stage.
In that year too they had a happy thought,
That little actresses were better taught.
But then, could six academies of arts
Prepare a Thorndike for a thousand parts?
Alice in Wonderland, or Nurse Cavell,
Judith or Joan or Jane – she rang the bell.
And all so rich, in vigour and in voice,
That even critics, who are deaf, rejoice.
(There is not much at which they have not grumbled,
But none has ever said 'Miss Thorndike mumbled').
Good work leaks out (let Youth be unafraid)
And queues of managers pursued the maid.
Ben Greet and Frohman helped the star to climb,
And other gentlemen before my time:
Old Vic – Young Binkie – Shakespeare – Mr Shaw –
Ibsen, they say, regarded her with awe.
And then, dear Sybil, you were never one
Who went on acting when the play was done.
A public friend, a very private wife,
A star not only of the stage but life,
Who else could cope with all the parts you bore –
Medea, Lady Macbeth – and 'Mother of Four'?
You've shown – and here you earn our best Hurrahs –
That mummers, after all, can be Mammas.
Let us salute the youngest of the old –
Her golden jubilee – our heart of gold.

For the celebrations, Sybil also did a scene as Elizabeth I from the still unproduced Dane play and then, as if to indicate that a golden jubilee certainly didn't mean retirement, she set off four weeks later on a massive recital tour of Australia and New Zealand accompanied by Lewis and John. As she was about to depart, the BBC decided that they too should

honour her fiftieth anniversary as an actress and did so with a radio production of *Henry VIII*. Olivier had two lines as the porter, in memory
of his original appearance as one of Sybil's train-bearers in the play, and
others gathered in the cast to do Sybil homage (she herself was of course
playing Queen Katharine) included Gielgud as Buckingham, Richardson
as Wolsey, Vivien Leigh as Ann Boleyn and Robert Donat as Cranmer.
Smaller parts were played by Lewis Casson, Richard Burton, Russell
Thorndike, Ernest Thesiger and Alan Webb. All in all, it wasn't a bad
send-off.

# 1954-1976

# 'Rarest and most blessed of women'

Sybil was now entering the last phase of her life. True, she had fully twenty years to live and all save the very last were to be active in one way or another, but the roles were now (with a very few exceptions) all variations on her more or less lovable old ladies and there were to be no more great surprises, no more stunning effects, only a hectic progress towards the twilight interrupted by increasingly frequent family and public celebrations of a long marriage, a long career and an even longer life.

Not that she herself would have seen her performances in these years as any kind of valedictory: for her, each one was a new start. First, in 1954, came the British Council tour of Australia and New Zealand on which the Cassons did poetry and prose extracts from around twenty authors all the way from Euripides to Dylan Thomas. They played in theatres, cinemas, hotel ballrooms, church halls, anywhere in fact that their manager Dan O'Connor could guarantee them an audience. This was the time when both Emlyn Williams and John Gielgud had established the box-office possibilities of recital shows, and for Sybil and Lewis (he now the proud holder of an honorary LL.D from Glasgow) there were the regulation two chairs and a table from which they held forth across the length and breadth of Australasia between other appearances at bazaars, tea parties and hospital functions.

This was, in all but name, a Royal tour and hugely successful, though their son John (who was with them), reckoned that, with his father now seventy-eight and his mother seventy-one, the Beatrice–Benedick wooing scenes were a little hard for some audiences to accept.

On then to India, where they examined the Taj Mahal and recited from Delhi to Darjeeling before returning to Australia via further recitals in Singapore and Hong Kong. They were bound back for Australia rather than England at this time because Ralph Richardson and Meriel Forbes had invited the Cassons to join them on a lengthy tour of two Rattigan plays, *The Sleeping Prince* and *Separate Tables*, Sybil to play the Grand

Duchess and Mrs Railton-Bell while Lewis was to be Northbrook in the first play and the old schoolmaster in the double-bill.

Thus the rest of 1955 was spent crossing and recrossing Australia and New Zealand, and from there the Cassons sailed for Durban to continue their recital tour through Africa. Then they travelled through Greece and on to Israel, still reciting, and by the time they did eventually get back to London Tennents had plans to put them both into T. S. Eliot's *The Family Reunion* which was to be part of the Scofield–Brook season at the Phoenix in the summer of 1956.

Reviews here were thoroughly mixed, divided between those critics who found Eliot an absorbing spiritual exercise and those who thought with Kenneth Tynan that:

though Mr Eliot can always lower the dramatic temperature, he can never raise it; and this is why the theatre, an impure assembly that loves strong emotions, must ultimately reject him. He is glacial, a theatrical Jack Frost; at the first breath of warmth, he melts and vanishes. This has-been, would-be masterpiece is magnificently revived by Peter Brook, however, who also designed the setting – an eerie upholstered vault. Apart from Mr Scofield, Sybil Thorndike as the doomed matriarch and Gwen Ffrangcon-Davies as Agatha the oracle perform magisterially, and fine work is done by Nora Nicolson and Patience Collier. The whole cast inhales Mr Eliot's thin air as if it were nourishing them; or as if it held some scent more refreshing than that of dry bones.

But Sybil didn't have much time to think about where she stood on the Eliot controversy. No sooner had she settled into the Phoenix than she began to spend her daytimes out at Pinewood filming for Olivier, playing the part she'd already played in Australia of the Grand Duchess in Rattigan's *The Sleeping Prince*. Only now it was called *The Prince and the Showgirl* and the stars were Olivier himself and Marilyn Monroe:

'Such a darling girl,' said Sybil, 'though always late on the set and terribly unhappy about something.' One morning, in the full and heavy coronation regalia of the Grand Duchess, Sybil was kept waiting by Miss Monroe for an hour before she arrived on the set and shooting could begin. Olivier made his co-star apologize to Dame Sybil: 'not at all', said Sybil, graciously accepting the apology. 'I'm sure we're all very glad to see you. Now that you are here, that is.'

Later, Sybil recalled:

When I started to play scenes with Marilyn I said to Larry, 'Does that get over, what she's doing? I can't hear a word she says. I think it's so underplayed.'

*133*

'Do you, dear?' he said; 'well, come and look at her in the rushes.' And I went to see them and of course she was perfect. I was the old ham. You see, Marilyn knew exactly what to do on the screen; I never did.

The filming was not exactly easy, and it dragged on until mid-November; its eventual release did not do much to enhance the careers of anyone involved, though since Miss Monroe's death interest in it has increased and of all Sybil's films it is the one most likely to reappear in retrospectives. In her postwar years Sybil was to make three more films after this one (*Alive and Kicking, Shake Hands with the Devil* and *Hand in Hand*) as well as one in Australia (*Smiley gets a Gun*), but the cinema, like television, remains at most a footnote to a talent which was perhaps too theatrical ever to thrive when mechanically reproduced.

Radio, though, was something else. Throughout the fifties and sixties the BBC encouraged her to recreate all her great stage roles, once in a sequence entitled *The Sybil Thorndike Festival*, and in a studio at Broadcasting House she felt very nearly as much at home as in the theatre, albeit unable ever to come to terms with the meaning of the flashing green 'on air' lights: 'Does that light mean I'm supposed to start speaking,' she once asked a surprised producer, 'or that I'm to stop?'

During the six-month run of *The Family Reunion* Sybil and Lewis had the offer to return to New York in another somewhat mystical play, Graham Greene's *The Potting Shed*. In what were to be their last Broadway appearances, Sybil played Mrs Callifer and Lewis was Dr Baston. They seem not to have got on especially well with their American director, but in all other respects this was a happy and distinguished if faintly muted farewell to the city where they had first appeared on stage in 1910.

From America they travelled back across the Pacific to Australia, where they'd had the offer of yet another tour – this time *The Chalk Garden* with their grand-daughter Jane Casson playing Laurel, Sybil as Mrs St Maugham (the part created in America by Dame Gladys Cooper and in London by Dame Edith Evans and the only one that all three were to play in the modern theatre) and Lewis as the Judge. This was also to be a kind of farewell (the Cassons were only to be seen again in Australia in recitals) and during the tour Lewis – now nearly eighty-three and running Shakespeare classes for the *Chalk Garden* company during the daytime as part of his unceasing struggle to maintain standards of verse-speaking among the younger members of his profession – had the fall on a flight of stairs which was to lead to his increasing blindness.

The Queen Dowager with Marilyn Monroe in Laurence Olivier's film *The Prince and The Showgirl*, 1957

Dora in Cyril Frankel's film *Alive and Kicking* with Estelle Winwood (*left*) and Kathleen Harrison (*right*), 1958

For the time being, though, all seemed well and by January 1959 they were back in the West End at the Globe in a new Clemence Dane comedy, *Eighty in the Shade*, which many viewed as a sort of celebration of the Cassons' golden wedding anniversary which duly occurred during the run. The rest of that year was taken up with radio and some television and film work (Sybil did *Riders to the Sea* for the BBC, while Lewis had an abortive flight to Rome where he was supposed to play Tiberius in *Ben-Hur* until on arrival he decided the chaos of that location was too great to allow him to contribute anything useful to the proceedings), and then came a tour of *The Sea Shell*, the first play that Sybil had done on stage without her husband since *Waters of the Moon* but in the event not one which ever reached London.

Work was now getting rather more scarce, Lewis's sight was failing fast, and there were worries about money – worries partly lifted in 1960 when they both got the offer to appear in *Waiting in the Wings*, Noël Coward's new play about a group of old actresses living out their enforced retirement at a home called The Wings in moods that ranged from open hostility, anger and bitterness at having to exist on charity, to contentment or at least fairly placid resignation.

Amazingly, Coward and the Cassons had never worked together before (though Sybil and Lewis had known him since the early twenties and had once taken some one-act plays of his out on tour) and they got on very well as rehearsals began for this curious, highly theatrical and often very effective blend of drama, pathos, humour and occasionally maudlin sentimentality: 'The play as a whole', wrote Coward later, 'contains the basic truth that old age needn't be nearly so dreary and sad as it's supposed to be, provided you greet it with humour and live it with courage' – a philosophy which didn't seem far removed from that of the Cassons in real life.

The new play, Coward's fiftieth, was turned down by H. M. Tennent (the management which had presented virtually all of his work in London since the war) and was eventually done at the Duke of York's under Michael Redgrave's auspices. It opened to cheers from the first-night audience followed by a mixed, sometimes vicious and generally hostile batch of reviews from newspapers still unenthusiastic about Coward's decision to live abroad for tax reasons. But the only really discordant note in the theatre was struck by a man from the *Express* asking Noël if there was any truth in the rumour that he'd had his face lifted several times, and despite the reviews Sybil and Lewis and Marie Löhr and the company

Marina in *Uncle Vanya* with Laurence Olivier as Astrov,
Chichester Festival Theatre, 1962

played to capacity for three months on the advance booking. Then however they went into a sharp pre-Christmas slump from which they never really recovered, though *Waiting in the Wings* (including tours before and after the London run) did survive for a total of very nearly nine months.

Immediately after the Coward play Sybil went into *Teresa of Avila*, an account by Hugh Ross Williamson of the saint whom Sybil was eager to see as 'a kind of mature Joan'. This the lady may well have been but the play certainly wasn't, and after a difficult tour they reached the Vaudeville in October 1961 only to close there in the first week of December.

Then, though Lewis was now nearly blind and Sybil at last beginning to feel her eighty years, they made one last visit to Australia for a recital tour which took them through the Spring of 1962; while they were there, Olivier had been appointed first director of the new Chichester Festival and he cabled inviting them to join him for a starry *Uncle Vanya*. Redgrave was in the title role with Olivier as Astrov, Joan Plowright as Sonya, Sybil as Marina and Lewis as Telyegin, the latter having to be prompted occasionally through an earpiece but still an infinitely powerful stage presence on the verge of his eighty-seventh birthday.

For this revival Sybil and Sir Laurence were recreating the roles they'd first played for the Vic at the New in 1945, and of Olivier's three productions that first year at Chichester this was the only real success – curiously perhaps, since it was the play least suited to the open stage. 'Genius', Clive Barnes called it in the *Express*, and the general feeling was that with this one star-laden achievement Olivier had not only rescued Chichester from a jolting start but had also established his right to move the company a year later to London as the founder members of the National Theatre Company. But though this *Vanya* did transfer to the Vic during their first season there in 1963, sadly Sybil was playing elsewhere at the time and neither she nor Lewis were to become members of the National company they had urged and argued into existence for the whole of their working lives.

From Chichester Sybil went first to Bristol where she celebrated her eightieth birthday in November 1962 singing and dancing (her début on the musical stage) in an otherwise unremarkable Julian Slade version of *Vanity Fair*. Lewis wasn't involved and took a generally dim view of the proceedings:

We still hope for the best, [he wrote from Bristol to his son in Australia] but I am finding it rather hard to keep boredom at bay. By myself mostly, and reading and writing mostly impossible. I don't get much out of going to the theatre when

With Athene Seyler and Derek
Farr in *Arsenic and Old Lace*,
Vaudeville Theatre, February
1966

With Lewis Casson examining
the model for Leatherhead's
new Thorndike Theatre, May
1967

we do go. You will have heard that some friends of mine have given me a new tape recorder and have done literary tapes for me – such a formidable collection, and I get a lot of pleasure from them. But alas I look the gift horse in the mouth by criticising the quality of the speech.

Lewis's gloom was echoed by the London critics when *Vanity Fair* reached the Queen's, but Sybil was wonderfully unrepentant: 'One should never be sorry one has attempted something new – never, never, never.' Offstage she was now spending more and more of her time reading aloud to Lewis, who could see very little indeed, but early in 1963 the two of them set off for a holiday in the Lake District ('Lewis fine and happy – so am I') and then both returned to Chichester for another brief season in *Vanya*.

~~Then, instead of going to the Vic with the new National company~~ Sybil, for reasons best known to herself, had another try at breathing life into Judith Guthrie's old play *Queen B*. This they toured briefly and unsuccessfully (Sybil as Lady Beatrice and Lewis as her butler) before Sybil got a rather better offer from William Douglas Home to go into *The Reluctant Peer*, playing the mother of the character the author had loosely based on his brother Sir Alec. If there was anything Sybil wasn't, it was an old Conservative dowager, but she played the Countess of Lister with relish until, in September 1964, she had to leave the cast to fulfil a promise to play in Arthur Marshall's adaptation of a Dorothy Malm novel, *Season of Goodwill*. This did not do, and nor did Sybil's next venture (*Return Ticket*), so that it was with some relief that she and Lewis sank gratefully into a revival of *Arsenic and Old Lace* at the Vaudeville. Lewis had just celebrated his ninetieth birthday and this efficient if shamefully mugged revival (with Athene Seyler and Sybil as the murderous old ladies and Lewis as their last victim) was to be the Cassons' last London play.

It ran through the first half of 1966 and then, in the late summer, Harold Hobson brought them an intriguing Marguerite Duras play called *The Viaduct*. Both were keen to play in it but Lewis came reluctantly to accept that he'd never manage to learn the lines and so, with Alan Webb in the part originally intended for him, Sybil opened at the Yvonne Arnaud in Guildford in January 1967. Other critics failed to share Hobson's enthusiasm, though, and the play closed after a short tour leaving Sybil and Lewis free to fly to Minneapolis for a holiday with their daughter Ann and son-in-law Douglas Campbell.

Back in England, they directed what was left of their remarkable energy towards the fund-raising for, and building of, the theatre in Leatherhead

The raising of the Thorndike banner,
Leatherhead, 1967

The last play: Sybil Thorndike in the
title role of John Graham's *There was
an Old Woman*, Thorndike Theatre,
Leatherhead, October 1969

that was to carry Sybil's name. At a cost of more than £350,000, much of it locally raised, the Thorndike Theatre was to be dedicated to Shaw's 'hard-hammered actress' and she herself would make a farewell appearance on its stage in October 1969.

For now however there was the 'breaking through' ceremony at which Lewis made a short speech, and Sybil then went out in a new though thoroughly unsuccessful Enid Bagnold play (*Call Me Jacky*) followed almost immediately by another long tour, this one in a revival of Emlyn Williams's *Night Must Fall*, remarkable only for the fact that it in, playing the brief role of the Judge, Lewis made his very last stage appearance in the middle of his ninety-third year.

In December of that year (1968) the Cassons celebrated their diamond wedding anniversary with a tremendous family gathering, the single most important happening in their lives since they'd been to Oxford together two years earlier to collect honorary doctorates.

The following May, Lewis died quietly in the Nuffield Hospital and Sybil, alone for the first time since they'd been married at Christmas 1908, now had only one more stage performance to give. It was, as she'd promised, at the Thorndike in Leatherhead which was formally opened in September and where a month later she played the homeless old crone who was the title figure in John Graham's *There was an Old Woman*. As a play and a farewell vehicle it left much to be desired, and never in fact got beyond Leatherhead; but as a choice of play (rather than some safe revival) it was hugely typical of Sybil and as a performance it has haunted all those who saw it. For three weeks the Thorndike was entirely sold out.

During the Leatherhead run Sybil had celebrated her eighty-seventh birthday and, although she still had nearly seven years to live, there were to be no more stage plays. There were however to be a large number of radio plays, television interviews, and frequent poetry recitals for the Apollo Society, as well as two National Portrait Gallery lectures (about Ellen Terry and Mrs Pankhurst), a Dickens recital in Westminster Abbey, a televised recital of her favourite prose and verse, Sunday-night readings for the Royal Commonwealth Institute and then a final stage appearance at Covent Garden on 3 January 1973 in the *Fanfare for Europe* which launched Britain's membership of the Common Market.

It was, typically, a retirement in name only and when in 1970 the news came that she was to be made a Companion of Honour, the highest distinction that the crown can give to an actress, that seemed only right and proper. In the whole history of the British theatre only two other women

had been made Companions, and they suitably were the two pioneers
of the repertory movement: Annie Horniman and Lilian Baylis. 'I can't
imagine', Olivier cabled Sybil when the announcement was made public,
'the Queen having a nicer Companion'.

Two years after that came the celebrations of her ninetieth birthday:
a gala performance at the Theatre Royal, Haymarket, with Sybil waving
from the Royal Box and turning the whole affair into a party, while on
stage a cast headed by Olivier, Richardson, Guinness, Scofield, Ustinov,
Edith Evans and Sybil's grand-daughter Jane Casson all gathered to do
their homage. Talking to Sybil at this time, in her Swan Court flat, I
asked if she had any real regrets:

Not many: sometimes I wish I didn't have such a temper, and I wish Lewis
and I hadn't had to quarrel so dreadfully, but then again I think that was so much
a part of us and our marriage that we couldn't have lived any other way. My
mother gave me a great zest for life, and my father made me know how important it was to love God and people, but they were a jolly strong and noisy couple
and I don't think I could ever have lived what you might call a quiet life.

I regret the pain I'm in now, with this bally arthritis, and I wish I were strong
enough to make it go away, and I get so cross that I can't do much, but I've
had a very long and healthy life so I can't really complain, now can I? Though
of course I do.

I suppose I regret the way the theatre has changed, the way that actors nowadays mumble and you can't often hear a word they say, but I can still hear Gielgud
and Richardson and Larry and they should be enough for anyone.

People always said I was just like Saint Joan, but I wasn't, you know; she was
the part I most enjoyed playing in all my life, and she was what I'd most have
liked to be, but I wasn't brave enough. Besides I'm a pacifist and she wasn't that,
now was she?

I find I dream a lot more than I used to, usually about a place near the sea
where there are great rocks and there's a long stretch of sand: whenever I have
that dream Lewis is always standing there, so I hope perhaps that's where we're
going in another life.

On the last day of February 1976 the National Theatre company bade
farewell to the Old Vic with an all-star performance of *Tribute to the Lady*,
a commemoration of Lilian Baylis in which the part of Sybil Thorndike
was played by Susan Fleetwood. But watching it from the stalls was Sybil
herself, and when at the end of the evening her presence there was
acknowledged by Peggy Ashcroft, the entire house rose and cheered. It
was her very last public appearance.

Then, on 9 June 1976, after two heart attacks within four days, Sybil Thorndike died at her flat in Swan Court: like Lewis, she had lived to celebrate her ninety-third birthday. 'She was', said Olivier in a tribute that night, 'one of the rarest and most blessed of women of whom this country could ever boast. The loss of her is incalculable.' *The Times* described her as one of the greatest and best-loved English actresses of the century, and for the *Guardian* Philip Hope-Wallace recalled Agate once saying that she had 'a heart as big as a railway station'.

Sybil Thorndike left £10,345 and theatrical treasures to various collections: she also banked in the hearts of those who knew her, on stage or off, a legacy of love and respect and often stunned admiration for the sheer tenacity of her life and work. For those of us who never saw her as Joan or Medea or Hecuba there are the recordings: imperfect, certainly, often incomplete and more than a little crackly, but add to their sound the memory of what she was like on stage even at the end – tireless, joyous, noisy and unashamed of going over the top just as Joan was unafraid of going over the bridge at Orleans – and you have a reasonably accurate image of what she must have been like.

Other actresses were as good as Sybil in many if not most of her other roles; but Joan was all hers and across fifty years no-one has ever quite managed to overtake or outdate her memory. She too, after all, had the faith.

On stage, her greatest gift was the one she shared with Olivier: total and utter fearlessness. Never one to play down or play safe, nor yet a great believer in the virtues of theatrical subtlety, she had to be seen on stage the way a display of fireworks has to be seen simply, in order to be believed. Not all of her performances were rockets, and the rain had got in at a few by the end, but by God she lit up the sky around a theatre. And you can't ask much more of an actress than that.

For a clergyman's daughter who started out to be a pianist, Sybil Thorndike was a miracle of versatility: yet those of us who knew her only at the end of her career, by which time the Greek and Shakespearian tragedy queen (a breed of actress always better appreciated in France than England) had mellowed into the 1950s and 1960s player of high comedy and *grande dame* roles, should not be in doubt about the steel that lay at the heart of all her acting. Sybil was nobody's fool; she may from time to time have made massive mistakes in the choice of plays and fellow players, yet she remained wonderfully conscious of her place in the theatre and of how it could best be maintained both on stage and off. 'Once,'

29 October 1972: *Sybil*, a ninetieth birthday tribute, Theatre Royal, Haymarket

said one of her co-stars in *Waters of the Moon*, 'Dame Edith was ill and we had to have an understudy on who wasn't nearly as good; but do you know an amazing thing? Dame Sybil seemed much happier that night.' I have long treasured that co-star's amazement, because it suggests that even her fellow players were unable to believe that Sybil could be subject to the normal laws of theatrical jealousy.

The fact that she was, and yet managed to rise above them and convince a huge number of people on both sides of the footlights that there was something more to acting than just the daily slog, is part of the key to her splendour. For the rest, you simply had to see her and, if your luck didn't run to that, look now at the pictures: look at the fire in the eyes, the determination in the line of the mouth, the set of the jaw. It's all there. Sybil took plays the way Joan took cities, by storm; the fact that they often couldn't withstand the attack wasn't entirely her fault.

Early in July 1976, with a fanfare of trumpets and in the presence of a standing-room-only congregation, her ashes were buried in Westminster Abbey at the end of a memorial service at which Ralph Richardson read the lesson, Paul Scofield read from *Cymbeline*, John Casson from *The Pilgrim's Progress* and John Gielgud gave an address which was in fact the best-written of all Dame Sybil's many obituaries. This book began with Gielgud on Thorndike, and that is perhaps also how it should now end:

Sybil Thorndike was the best-loved English actress since Ellen Terry and these two great players shared many of the same fine qualities – generosity, diligence, modesty, simplicity.

Both were demons for hard work – Ellen Terry called it her blessèd work but that could be taken with two different meanings, for she often longed (or said she longed) to live in the country and forget the theatre. But her private life was not destined to bring her great happiness, and she was a somewhat tragic figure in her old age.

It was quite otherwise with Sybil Thorndike. The theatre was the breath of life to her – the theatre, music and her deep religious faith.

Blessed with immense talent, boundless energy, unremitting application and splendid health – until the last few years when she learned to triumph over continual pain and increasing disabilities – she fought her way, helped by the devotion of a brilliant husband and loving family, to worldwide recognition.

Her good works were manifold, her influence for good shone from her like a beacon, but she hated to be praised and to be thought sweet and saintly. 'I hate pathos,' she said once. 'It's soft and weak. But tragedy has fight.'

In Lewis Casson she had a superb partner and a tremendous fighter, though his temperament was often inclined to be moody and pessimistic in contrast to Sybil's radiant determination to see the best in everyone and everything around her. He argued with her endlessly, criticised her ruthlessly, and tried to control some of the more eccentric enthusiasms and outbursts of exaggeration which sometimes tended to mar her acting.

Outrageous she could certainly be at times, playing to the hilt a second-rate play which gave her an opportunity to let off steam in some particular repulsive or wildly melodramatic character. But Sybil would be the first to admit, with a hoot of laughter, that, it was all such fun, and apologise ruefully for overacting at a matinée with the excuse that a cherished grandchild had been in front.

In her long life there was no moment wasted, never a thought of boredom, laziness or surfeit. Sybil, someone said, had no airs, only graces. She was perfectly at ease with Royalty, poets, politicians or men of letters, and equally natural sitting on the doorstep of a miner's cottage in Wales, chatting to the wives and telling them the story of Medea. But you would hardly expect to find her at Wimbledon or Ascot; more probably at home, doing piano scales and voice exercises, learning a new part, studying a new language, reading aloud to her grandchildren, or arguing furiously with Lewis.

Intensely feminine in her maternal and womanly qualities, she could not, on the stage, be coquettish or swooningly romantic: she never attempted Juliet or Cleopatra. 'I can't be sheer femininity,' she said. 'Feminine wiles I can't manage and I don't want to!'

She was very fine (though to my mind, unequal) in her playing of tragedy, but she was the only actress of her generation to dare even to attempt it. She took the stage, whether as Lady Macbeth, Queen Katharine or Hecuba, with a splendid stride, faultless phrasing and diction, and riveted her audiences with her superb authority and vocal power. In comedy, she was sometimes tempted to hit too hard, but as the years passed her skill and control, under Lewis' iron hand, restrained and refined the execution of her art to a marked degree.

*Saint Joan* of course was written for her, and it was her acting masterpiece as well as Shaw's greatest play, though she must have got sick and tired of hearing people say so. Her performance was unrivalled. Here she did not need to play for sheer femininity, nor for masculinity either. Her tearing up of the renunciation in the trial scene was a moment of really great acting that I shall never forget, but she was as convincing in the slangy colloquial passages as in the great poetic speeches, blending the different sides of the character with unerring judgement, and never for a moment allowing sentimentality or sanctimoniousness to intrude on the simple directness of her drive.

In her private life she managed somehow to retain a certain reserve and dignity, despite an ebullient facade. She had beautiful manners. She was genuinely interested in everyone she met, strangers as well as friends. She could bounce and flounce without ever losing her modesty and basic humility. The moment you were lucky enough to work with her in the theatre you knew she was a leader, a giver, never self-centred – professional to her fingertips, disciplined, punctual, kind. She confessed to having a terrible temper but I never saw a sign of it myself.

To me the most perfect examples of her playing were in some of the comparatively restrained performances in which she displayed her essential womanliness – Jane Clegg, Miss Moffat in *The Corn is Green*, the Mothers in *The Distaff Side* and *The Linden Tree*, and her lovely acting in the two Hunter plays, *Waters of the Moon* and *A Day by the Sea*.

'When Lewis died,' she said, 'I became a bit tired of myself.' But we could never tire of her, as we watched her rallying her forces in those last splendid years, still eager to understand new styles, to appreciate new talents, to lend shrewd advice and criticism, fearlessly honest about everything she saw and read.

Her beauty grew, as it had every right to do, in her old age, and her noble head, veiled in the white scarf she always came to wear, picked her out in any gathering, whether at theatres or parties or in church, as she listened and watched and walked, more slowly now, with an unerring sense of any occasion which she was honouring with her presence.

'O Lewis,' she cried once, 'if only we could be the first actors to play on the moon.' That was Sybil Thorndike-Casson: simple and loving in her private life, noble and beautiful in her public ways.

# Stage Performances

1904

May
Dolly Clandon in *You Never Can Tell* by Bernard Shaw, King's Hall, Covent Garden (Romany Amateur Dramatic Club)

June
Toured with Ben Greet's Company of Pastoral Players. She first appeared on the afternoon of 14 June as Palmis in *The Palace of Truth* by W. S. Gilbert, acted in the grounds of Downing College, Cambridge. That evening she walked on in scenes from *The Merry Wives of Windsor*. On 18 June, at a matinée in the garden of Worcester College, Oxford, she created her first part in a new play, Phyllis, in H. M. Paull's *My Lord from Town*

September 1904–
1907
With the Ben Greet company in Shakespeare and Old Comedy in the United States, playing a swarm of lesser parts (including 'Lucianus, nephew to the King' in *Hamlet* and Ceres in *The Tempest*) and occasionally such parts as Viola, Helena, Gertrude, Rosalind, Ophelia, Nerissa, and (Kansas City, 1905) Everyman. Acted 112 parts in all, not counting Noises Off

December 1907
O Chicka San in *His Japanese Wife*, one-act play by Grace Griswold, Bijou, Bedford Street, London

1908

February
Janet Morice in *The Marquis* by Cecil Raleigh and Sidney Dark, Scala (Play Actors)

Spring tour
Understudied Candida in Bernard Shaw's play (tour opened at Belfast) and acted Kezia in curtain-raiser, *The Subjection of Kezia* by Mrs Havelock Ellis

Summer
Seasons in pastoral plays

149

| | |
|---|---|
| August | Candida in Gaiety, Manchester, company on tour |
| *September 1908–*<br>*May 1909* | With Miss Horniman's company at the Gaiety Theatre, Manchester, playing:<br>Bessie in *Marriages Are Made in Heaven* by Basil Dean<br>Mrs Rawlings in *When The Devil Was Ill* by Charles McEvoy<br>Caroline Blizzard in *Gentlemen of the Road* by Charles McEvoy (one-act play)<br>Lady Denison in *The Charity That Began at Home* by St John Hankin<br>Mrs Chartoris in *His Helpmate* by Charles McEvoy (one-act play)<br>Mrs Barthwick in *The Silver Box* by John Galsworthy<br>Artemis in the *Hippolytus* by Euripides (Gilbert Murray version)<br>Nurse Price in *Cupid and the Styx* by J. Sackville Martin<br>Thora in *The Feud* by Edward Garnett<br>Gertrude Eckersley in *Trespassers Will Be Prosecuted* by M. A. Arabian<br>Bettina in *The Vale of Content (Das Glück im Winkel)* by Hermann Sudermann |
| *June 1909* | In Gaiety Theatre company's season, Coronet, London |
| *1910*<br>January | Sal Fortescue in *Peg Woffington's Pearls* by C. Duncan Jones and Dennis Cleugh, Court (Play Actors) |
| February | Columbine in *The Marriage of Columbine* by Harold Chapin, Court (Play Actors) |
| March–June | With Charles Frohman's Repertory company, Duke of York's, London, appearing as:<br>Winifred in *The Sentimentalists* by George Meredith<br>Emma Huxtable in *The Madras House* by Granville Barker<br>Romp in *Prunella* by Granville Barker and Laurence Housman<br>Maggie Massey in *Chains* by Elizabeth Baker |
| September | Emily Chapman in *Smith* by W. Somerset Maugham, Empire Theatre, New York |

*1911*

Spring and
Summer     Touring North America in *Smith*

*1912*

June     Beatrice Farrar in *Hindle Wakes* by Stanley Houghton,
Aldwych (Miss Horniman's Gaiety, Manchester, company under Stage Society auspices)

July     Beatrice in *Hindle Wakes*, Playhouse (for first weeks of
regular run) and Dolly in *Makeshift* by Gertrude Robins

*August 1912–*
*May 1913*     With Gaiety Theatre, Manchester, company, appear-
ing as:
Jennie Rollins in *The Question* (one-act play) by John
J. Wickham
Mrs Eversleigh in *The Charity That Began at Home* by
St John Hankin
Renie Dalrymple in *Revolt* by George Calderon
Malkin in *The Whispering Well* by Frank H. Rose
Jane Clegg in *Jane Clegg* by St John Ervine
Romp in *Prunella* by Granville Barker and Laurence
Housman
Privacy in *Prunella* (second production)

*1913*

May     Played Jane Clegg, Ann Wellwyn, and Lady Philox in
Harold Chapin's *Elaine* at the Court Theatre, London
(with Gaiety Theatre company)

September–
October     At Gaiety, Manchester, playing:
Annie Scott in *The Price of Thomas Scott* by Elizabeth
Baker
Miss Stormit in *Nothing Like Leather* (one-act) by Allan
Monkhouse
Hester Dunnybrig in *The Shadow* by Eden Phillpotts
Portia in *Julius Caesar* by William Shakespeare

October     Hester in *The Shadow*, Court Theatre, London (with
Gaiety Theatre company)

*November 1914–*
*May 1918*  A member of the Old Vic company (producer for Lilian Baylis: Ben Greet). Her first performance was Adriana in *The Comedy of Errors* on 30 November 1914 During her four seasons at the Vic she played for the first time in England:

Lady Macbeth in *Macbeth*
Rosalind in *As You Like It*
Portia in *The Merchant of Venice*
Constance in *King John*
Beatrice in *Much Ado About Nothing*
Imogen in *Cymbeline*
Chorus and Katharine in *Henry the Fifth*
Julia in *The Two Gentlemen of Verona*
Ophelia in *Hamlet*
Queen Margaret in *Richard the Third*
Mrs Ford in *The Merry Wives of Windsor*
Besides nearly all the principal female characters in the plays of Shakespeare, she appeared also as:
Prince Hal in *Henry IV, Part I*
The Fool in *King Lear*
Ferdinand in *The Tempest*
Launcelot Gobbo in *The Merchant of Venice*
Rugby in *The Merry Wives of Windsor*
Puck in *A Midsummer Night's Dream*
also such parts as:
Lady Teazle in *The School for Scandal* by Sheridan
Kate Hardcastle in *She Stoops to Conquer* by Oliver Goldsmith
Lydia Languish in *The Rivals* by Sheridan
Peg Woffington in *Masks and Faces* by Charles Reade and Tom Taylor
Columbine in *The Sausage String's Romance; or, A New Cut Harlequinade* by Russell Thorndike, Geoffrey Wilkinson, and Sybil Thorndike
During her stay at the Vic she appeared in *The Winter's Tale* section of the Shakespeare Pageant, part of the Shakespeare Tercentenary matinée at Drury Lane (2 May 1916). She also went with the Old Vic company

to Stratford-upon-Avon where it fulfilled the Summer Festival at the Shakespeare Memorial Theatre during August 1916; nine plays of Shakespeare, two of Sheridan, one of Goldsmith. In the early summer of 1917 the company had a season at Portsmouth, followed by three weeks of twice-nightly performances during which she appeared as Nancy in *Oliver Twist*

*1918*

June       Mrs Lopez in *The Profiteers*, adapted by Walter Hackett from the one-act French play (*Gonzague*) of Pierre Veber, London Pavilion (in a Variety bill)

Françoise Regnard in *The Kiddies in the Ruins* (*Les Gosses dans les Ruines*) adapted from the French of Paul Gsell and Francisque Poulbot by Brigadier-General J. E. Cannot and introduced into Cochran's 'Fragment from France', *The Better 'Ole*, New Oxford Theatre, London

December       Understudying Madge Titheradge as Eugénie in *In The Night Watch* adapted by Michael Morton from the French, New Oxford Theatre, London

*1919*

March       Sygne de Coûfontaine in *The Hostage* by Paul Claudel, translated by Pierre Chavannes, Scala Theatre (Pioneer Players)

April       Naomi Melsham in *The Chinese Puzzle* by Marion Bower and Leon M. Lion (Sybil Thorndike took Ethel Irving's place), New Theatre

July       Dr James Barry in *Dr James Barry* by Olga Racster and Jessica Grove, St James's (matinée)

July 4       Court matinée (no specified item on programme)

September       Clara Borstwick in *The Great Day* by Louis N. Parker and George R. Sims, Drury Lane

October       Hecuba in *The Trojan Women* by Euripides, translated by Gilbert Murray, Old Vic (matinées)

Anne Wickham in *Napoleon* by Herbert Trench, Queen's (Stage Society)

November       Śakuntalá in *Śakuntalá* by Kálidasá, Laurence Binyon's version adapted for the stage by K. N. Das Gupta, Winter Garden (matinée)

| | |
|---|---|
| December | Hecuba in *The Trojan Women*, Old Vic and Holborn Empire (matinées) |
| *1920*<br>February–<br>March | Hecuba, Candida, Medea (in Gilbert Murray's version of the *Medea* of Euripides), Holborn Empire (matinées) |
| March | Mary Hey in *Tom Trouble* by John Burley, Holborn Empire (matinées) |
| April | Beryl Napier in *The Showroom* by Lady Bell, Holborn Empire (matinées) |
| May | Mathilde Stangerson in *The Mystery of the Yellow Room* adapted from Gaston Leroux's play by Hannaford Bennett, St James's |
| June | Céline in *The Children's Carnival* translated by Christopher St John from *Carnaval des Enfants* by Saint-Georges de Bouhélier, Kingsway (Pioneer Players) |
| *September 1920–*<br>*June 1922* | Grand Guignol seasons at the Little Theatre. Appeared in the following parts in various programmes:<br>Carmen in *G.H.Q. Love* from the French of Pierre Rehm<br>Elise Charrier in *The Hand of Death* by André de Lorde and Alfred Binet<br>Lea in *Private Room No. 6* by André de Lorde<br>Cinders, 'with song and dance', in *Oh, Hell!!!*, by Reginald Arkell and Russell Thorndike<br>Marcelle in *The Medium* by Pierre Mille and C. de Vylar, adapted by José G. Levy<br>Judy in *The Tragedy of Mr Punch* by Russell Thorndike and Reginald Arkell<br>Daisy in *The Person Unknown* by H. F. Maltby<br>Liz in *The Love Child* by Frederick Fenn and Richard Pryce<br>Catherine in *The Kill* by Maurice Level, adapted by W. H. Harris<br>The Girl in *The Chemist* by Max Maurey, adapted by Blanche Weiner<br>She in *The Vigil* by André de Lorde |

Louise in *The Old Women* by André de Lorde, adapted by Christopher Holland

The Wife in *The Unseen* by J. J. Renaud, adapted by Lewis Casson

Chou Chou in *Crime* by Maurice Level, adapted by Lewis Casson

Millicent Wentworth in *Amends* by E. Crawshay-Williams

Mrs Forrest in *Changing Guard* by W. G. Nott-Bower

Katie Cripps in *De Mortuis* by Stanley Logan

Stephanie Meyrick in *Cupboard Love* by E. Crawshay-Williams

Amelia Angelfield in *Amelia's Suitors; or, Colonel Chutney's First Defeat* by H. F. Maltby

Rosalie in *The Nutcracker Suite* by E. Crawshay-Williams

Mrs Meldon in *Progress* by St John Ervine

His Betrothed in *Rounding the Triangle* by E. Crawshay-Williams

Madame Jeanne Chabrin in *The Unseen* by J. J. Renaud, adapted by Lewis Casson

The Shop Girl in *The Old Story* by C. H. Hirsch, adapted by Hugh McLellan

The Girl in *Fear* by André de Lorde

*1921*

April     Mother Sawyer in *The Witch of Edmonton* by Thomas Dekker, John Ford, and William Rowley, Lyric, Hammersmith (Stage Society)

June     Lady Macbeth in *Macbeth* by Shakespeare, Odéon, Paris

November     Evadne in *The Maid's Tragedy* by Beaumont and Fletcher, Lyric Theatre, Hammersmith (Phoenix Society)

December     Lady Wrathie in *Shall We Join the Ladies?* by J. M. Barrie, Palace (King George's Pension Fund performance)

*1922*

April 27     An old lady in *Thirty Minutes in the Street* by Bertie Meyer, Kingsway (Playwrights Theatre); repeated Palace, 27 June (charity matinée)

| | |
|---|---|
| May | Hecuba in *The Trojan Women* at the Palace (matinée) and at Drury Lane (matinée for Newspaper Press Fund) |
| July | Jane in *Jane Clegg* by St John Ervine, New |
| | Tosca in excerpt from *La Tosca* by Sardou, Coliseum |
| September | Charlotte Fériol in *Scandal* by Lady Bell from the French of Henry Bataille, New |
| October | *Medea*, New (matinée) |
| November | Beatrice in *The Cenci* by Percy Bysshe Shelley, New |

### 1923

| | |
|---|---|
| January | April Mawne in *Advertising April* by Herbert Farjeon and Horace Horsnell, Criterion |
| June | Provincial tour in ~~*Scandal, Advertising April, Jane Clegg,*~~ and *Medea* |
| September | Imogen in *Cymbeline* by William Shakespeare, New |
| October | Elinor Shale in *The Lie* by Henry Arthur Jones, New |

### 1924

| | |
|---|---|
| January | Gruach in *Gruach* by Gordon Bottomley, St Martin's (Playbox; matinées) |
| March | Joan in *Saint Joan* by Bernard Shaw, New |
| May | Sonia in *Man and the Masses* by Ernst Toller, adapted by Louis Untermeyer, New (Stage Society) |
| July | Rosalind in *As You Like It*, Regent (Fellowship of Players) |
| October | Hecuba in *The Trojan Women* (matinée), New |

### 1925

| | |
|---|---|
| January | Joan in *Saint Joan*, Regent, King's Cross |
| February | Phaedra and Artemis in the *Hippolytus* of Euripides (Gilbert Murray version), Regent |
| March | Claire in *The Verge* by Susan Glaspell, Regent (Pioneer Players) |
| May | Daisy Drennan in *The Round Table* by Lennox Robinson, Wyndham's |
| | Elinor Shale in *The Lie* by Henry Arthur Jones, Wyndham's |
| June | Medea, Peckwater Quad, Christ Church, Oxford (matinée) |

December        Queen Katharine in *Henry the Eighth* by William Shakespeare, Empire

**1926**

March        Beatrice in *The Cenci* by Shelley, Empire
                     Joan in *Saint Joan*, Lyceum

April        The Duchesse de Croucy in *Israel* by Henry Bernstein, adapted by Sidney C. Isaacs, Strand (matinée)
                     Gertrude in *Hamlet*, Lyceum (for Sadler's Wells Fund)

June        Judith in *Granite* by Clemence Dane, Ambassadors

July        Helen Stanley in *The Debit Account* by Eliot Crawshay-Williams, New (Interlude Players)
                     The Tragic Muse in the Garrick Pageant of 1769, recreated by R. Crompton Rhodes, Stratford-upon-Avon

December        Lady Macbeth in *Macbeth*, Princes

**1927**

February        Nadejda Ivanovna Pestoff in *The Greater Love* by J. B. Fagan, Princes

March        Angela Guiseley in *Angela* by Lady Bell, Princes

April        Medea in the *Medea* of Euripides (Gilbert Murray version), Princes

June        *Saint Joan* and *Medea* at the Théâtre des Champs-Elysées, Paris

**September 1927–**
**January 1928**        With the Old Vic company at the Lyric, Hammersmith, playing:
                     Katharina in *The Taming of the Shrew*
                     Portia in *The Merchant of Venice*
                     Beatrice in *Much Ado About Nothing*
                     Chorus and Katharine in *Henry the Fifth*

**1928**

February        Judith in *Judith of Israel*, based by E. de Marnay Baruch upon the Apocryphal Book of Judith, Strand
                     Tour with scenes from *Henry V*

April        Everyman in *Everyman*, Rudolf Steiner Hall
                     Queen Elizabeth in *The Making of an Immortal* by George Moore, Arts

Rosamund Withers in *The Stranger in the House* by Michael Morton and Peter Traill, Wyndham's

|  |  |
|---|---|
| *Summer 1928–*<br>*Spring 1929* | Toured South Africa as:<br>Elinor Shale in *The Lie*<br>Jane in *Jane Clegg*<br>Chorus and Katharine in *Henry the Fifth*<br>Beatrice in *Much Ado About Nothing*<br>Lady Macbeth in *Macbeth*<br>Joan in *Saint Joan*<br>Mrs Phelps in *The Silver Cord* by Sidney Howard |

*1929*

| | |
|---|---|
| March | Barbara Undershaft in *Major Barbara* by Bernard Shaw, Wyndham's |
| April | Lily Cobb in *Mariners* by Clemence Dane, Wyndham's<br>Lady Rathie in *Shall We Join The Ladies?* by J. M. Barrie, 28 April, Ellen Terry Memorial Matinée, Palace |
| May | Jane Clegg in *Jane Clegg* and Medea in *Medea* (the two plays in one evening), Wyndham's |
| June | Lady Lassiter in *The Donkey's Nose* by Eliot Crawshay-Williams, Prince of Wales's (Sunday Play Society) |
| December | Madame de Beauvais (Citizeness Pawnbroker) in *Madame Plays Nap* by Brenda Girvin and Monica Cozens, New |

*1930*

| | |
|---|---|
| January | Dorothy Lister in *The Devil* by Benn W. Levy, Arts |
| February | Ronnie's Mother in *To Meet the King* by H. C. G. Stevens (one-act), London Coliseum |
| March | Phèdre in *Phèdre* by Racine (in French), Arts<br>Sylvette in *The Fire in the Opera House* by Georg Kaiser, Everyman, Hampstead |
| April | Mrs Alving in *Ghosts* by Henrik Ibsen, Everyman, Hampstead |
| May | Emilia in *Othello*, Savoy |
| August | Began provincial tour as:<br>Dolores Mendez in *The Squall* by Jean Bart |

Mrs Alving in *Ghosts* by Henrik Ibsen
Jess Fortune in *The Matchmaker* by Ashley Dukes (later
re-titled *Matchmaker's Arms*)
Judith in *Granite*

**1931**

March
:   Marcelle in *The Medium* by Pierre Mille and C. de
Vylar, adapted by J. G. Levy, Palladium

April
:   Joan in *Saint Joan*, His Majesty's
Monica Wilmot in *Dark Hester* by Walter Ferris (per-
formance in aid of Middlesex Hospital), New

May
:   Eloise Fontaine in *Marriage by Instalments* by Steve Pass-
eur, adapted by Jocelyn Clive, Embassy

**1932**

January
:   The Citizen's Wife in *The Knight of the Burning Pestle*,
by Beaumont and Fletcher, Old Vic

February
:   Julie Renaudin in *The Dark Saint* by François de Curel,
adapted by Barbara Ling, Fortune

February
:   In Egypt and Palestine

April
:   Australasian tour as:
Joan in *Saint Joan*
Lady Macbeth in *Macbeth*
Madame de Beauvais in *Madame Plays Nap*
Lady Cicely Waynflete in *Captain Brassbound's Con-
version* by Bernard Shaw
April in *Advertising April*
Judith in *Granite*
Kitty Fane in *The Painted Veil* by W. Somerset Maug-
ham
Gertrude Rhead in *Milestones* by Arnold Bennett and
Edward Knoblock

**1933**

September
:   Reappeared in London as:
Evie Millward in *The Distaff Side* by John Van Druten,
Apollo

November
:   Mrs Siddons in *Mrs Siddons* by Naomi Royde Smith,
Apollo (matinée)

Queen Katharine in 'a dramatic entertainment' in aid of the Actors' Church Union, Seaford House, Belgrave Square

**1934**

| | |
|---|---|
| March | Victoria Van Brett in *Double Door* by Elizabeth McFadden, Globe |
| May | Nourmahal in *Aureng-Zebe*, heroic tragedy by John Dryden, Westminster |
| June | A Passenger, 'Z', in *Village Wooing* by Bernard Shaw, Little |
| September | Evie Millward in *The Distaff Side*, Booth, New York |

**1935**

| | |
|---|---|
| June | Blanche Oldham in *Grief Goes Over* by Merton Hodge, Globe |
| November | Lady Bucktrout in *Short Story* by Robert Morley, Queen's |
| | Emilia in *Othello* (Act V, Scene 2), National Theatre Appeal Matinée, Drury Lane |
| December | Lisha Gerart in *The Farm of Three Echoes* by Noel Langley, Wyndham's (1930 Players) |

**1936**

| | |
|---|---|
| June | Mary Herries in *Kind Lady* by Edward Chodorov, from a story by Hugh Walpole, Lyric |
| August | Toured as: |
| | Mrs Gascoigne in *My Son, My Son*, unrevised play by D. H. Lawrence, completed by Walter Greenwood |
| | Lady Maureen Gilpin in *Hands Across the Sea* by Noël Coward |
| | Doris Gow in *Fumed Oak* by Noël Coward |
| | 'Z' in *Village Wooing* by Bernard Shaw |
| December | Aphrodite and the Nurse in the *Hippolytus* of Euripides, Streatham Hill |

**1937**

| | |
|---|---|
| Spring | Toured as Betsy Loveless in *Six Men of Dorset* by Miles Malleson |
| June | Ann Murray in *Yes, My Darling Daughter* by Mark Reed, St James's |

December      Hecuba in *The Trojan Women* of Euripides, Adelphi (matinée)

*1938*
January      Mrs Conway in *Time and the Conways* by J. B. Priestley, Ritz, New York

April      Volumnia in *Coriolanus* by Shakespeare, Old Vic

September      Miss Moffat in *The Corn is Green* by Emlyn Williams, Duchess

*1940–1942*      Toured mining villages and towns for CEMA as: Lady Macbeth, Medea, and Candida

*1941*
March 12      Joan in *Saint Joan*, Palace (charity matinée)

July      Constance in *King John* by Shakespeare, New Theatre (Old Vic company)

Medea in the *Medea* of Euripides, New

*1942*      Further tour for CEMA in previous parts and also as Rebekah and Chorus in *Jacob*, by Laurence Housman, for the Old Vic

Georgina Jeffreys in *The House of Jeffreys* by Russell Thorndike, Playhouse

*1943*
March      Appeared at Gaiety Theatre, Dublin as:
Mrs Alving in *Ghosts* by Henrik Ibsen
Lady Cicely in *Captain Brassbound's Conversion* by Bernard Shaw
Mrs Hardcastle in *She Stoops to Conquer* by Oliver Goldsmith
Mrs Hardcastle at Theatre Royal, Bristol

May      Lady Beatrice in *Queen B* by Judith Guthrie, Theatre Royal, Bristol

July      Mrs Dundass in *Lottie Dundass* by Enid Bagnold, Vaudeville

November      Appeared in *The Rape of the Locks* by Menander, Queen Mary Hall

December      Queen of Hearts and White Queen in *Alice in Wonderland* and *Alice Through the Looking-Glass* adapted from Lewis Carroll's books by Clemence Dane, Scala

*1944*

February 20      Ronnie's mother in *To Meet The King* by H. C. G. Stevens, London Hippodrome (Green Room Rag)

Spring      Toured the Orkneys and Shetlands in Dramatic Poetry Recitals

August      With the Old Vic company at the New Theatre appeared as:

Aase in *Peer Gynt* by Ibsen, adapted by Norman Ginsbury

Catherine Petkoff in *Arms and the Man* by Bernard Shaw

Queen Margaret in *Richard the Third* by Shakespeare

December      Again in *Alice in Wonderland*, Palace (mornings only)

*1945*

January      Marina, the Nurse, in *Uncle Vanya* by Anton Tchehov (Constance Garnett version), New

Toured for ENSA with the Old Vic company in Germany, Belgium, and France, and also appeared at the Comédie Française

*September 1945–*
*April 1946*      With the Old Vic company at the New Theatre as:

Mistress Quickly in *Henry IV*, *Parts I and II* by Shakespeare

Jocasta in *Oedipus Rex*, by Sophocles, translated by W. B. Yeats

The Justice's Lady in *The Critic* by R. B. Sheridan

*1946*

May      Mrs Woodrow Wilson (Edith Bolling Wilson) in *In Time to Come* by Howard Koch and John Huston, King's Theatre, Hammersmith

June      Clytemnestra in the *Electra* of Euripides (Gilbert Murray version), King's Theatre, Hammersmith

*1947*

April      Mrs Fraser in *Call Home the Heart* by Clemence Dane, St James's

August            Isobel Linden in *The Linden Tree* by J. B. Priestley,
                  Duchess

*1948*
  November        Mrs Jackson in *The Return of the Prodigal* by St John
                  Hankin, Globe

*1949*
  February        Isabel Brocken in *The Foolish Gentlewoman* by Margery
                  Sharp, Duchess
  September       Aunt Anna Rose in *Treasure Hunt* by M. J. Farrell and
                  John Perry, Apollo
  November        Murder Scene from *Macbeth*, with Lewis Casson, '. . .
                  Merely Players', London Coliseum (Sunday evening)

*1950*
  August          Lady Randolph in *Douglas* by John Home, Lyceum,
                  Edinburgh (Edinburgh Festival); produced also at
                  Citizens' Theatre, Glasgow

*1951*
  April           Mrs Whyte in *Waters of the Moon* by N. C. Hunter,
                  Haymarket
  July            Spoke John Masefield's Ode at the foundation stone-
                  laying of the National Theatre (by HM the Queen, now
                  HM the Queen-Mother) on 13 July
  October         In *No Hurry, Ifor Davies*, a fantasy by Emlyn Williams
                  in *Salute to Ivor Novello*, London Coliseum (Sunday
                  evening)

*1952*
  March           Spoke the Prologue to '. . . Merely Players', in the per-
                  son of Mrs Siddons, Drury Lane

*1953*
  April           Queen Katherine in *Henry VIII* (Act III, Scene I),
                  Adelphi (Green Room Rag)
  November        Laura Anson in *A Day by the Sea* by N. C. Hunter, Hay-
                  market

*1954*

February–

March   Appeared in reading of *Under Milk Wood* by Dylan Thomas, Old Vic (two Sunday performances)

May 31   Queen Elizabeth I in a scene from *The Lion and the Unicorn* by Clemence Dane at Matinée for Golden Jubilees of Dame Sybil Thorndike and RADA and the centenary of Sir Herbert Tree's birth, Her Majesty's

Summer   Began extensive tour of Australia, New Zealand, Tasmania, India, Hong Kong, Malaya, in poetry recitals with Lewis Casson. Programmes included scenes from the *Medea, Saint Joan, The Trojan Women, Macbeth, Henry V, Much Ado About Nothing, Henry VIII, Twelfth Night, The Taming of the Shrew, The Winter's Tale, The Lion and the Unicorn*, etc., and many poems and ballads, early English to Dylan Thomas

*1955*

Spring–

March 1956   Australasian tour as:

Her Imperial and Royal Highness the Grand Duchess Charles in *The Sleeping Prince* by Terence Rattigan

Mrs Railton-Bell in *Separate Tables* by Terence Rattigan

*1956*

Toured South Africa, Rhodesia, Kenya, Israel and Turkey with Lewis Casson in dramatic recitals

June   Amy, Lady Monchensey in *The Family Reunion* by T. S. Eliot, Phoenix Theatre

July   Narrator, Ellen Terry Memorial Performance, Barn Theatre, Smallhythe

October   *Façade* (poetry reading), Light Opera Group, Scala

*1957*

January   Mrs Callifer in *The Potting Shed* by Graham Greene, Bijou Theatre, New York

*1957–8*

Toured Australia and New Zealand as Mrs St Maugham in *The Chalk Garden* by Enid Bagnold and poetry readings

**1959**

January      Dame Sophia Carrell in *80 in the Shade* by Clemence Dane, Globe Theatre

July      Poetry readings, Ellen Terry Memorial Performance, Barn Theatre, Smallhythe

October      Toured as Mrs Kittridge in *The Sea Shell* by Jess Gregg

**1960**

September      Lotta Bainbridge in *Waiting in the Wings* by Noël Coward, Duke of York's Theatre

**1961**

October      Teresa in *Teresa of Avila* by Hugh Ross Williamson, Vaudeville Theatre

**1962**

     Toured Australia in poetry recitals with Lewis Casson

July      Marina in *Uncle Vanya*, Chichester Festival Theatre

November      Miss Crawley in *Vanity Fair* by Julian Slade, Bristol Old Vic and Queen's Theatre

**1963**

July      Marina in *Uncle Vanya*, Chichester Festival Theatre

September      Lady Cuffe in *Queen B* by Judith Guthrie, Theatre Royal, Windsor and tour

**1964**

January      Dowager Countess of Lister in *The Reluctant Peer* by William Douglas-Home, Duchess

September      Mrs Storch in *Season of Goodwill* by Arthur Marshall, Queen's

**1965**

March      Mrs Doris Tate in *Return Ticket* by William Corlett, Duchess

**1966**

February      Abby Brewster in *Arsenic and Old Lace*, Vaudeville

**1967**

January      Claire Ragond in *The Viaduct* by Marguerite Duras, Yvonne Arnaud, Guildford, and tour

*1968*

February         Mrs Basil in *Call Me Jacky* by Enid Bagnold, Yvonne
                 Arnaud, Guildford

April            Mrs Bramson in *Night Must Fall* by Emlyn Williams,
                 national tour

*1969*

September        The Woman in *There was an Old Woman* by John Gra-
                 ham, Thorndike, Leatherhead

*1973*

January          Appeared in *Fanfare for Europe*, Royal Opera House,
                 Covent Garden

*Sybil*, a gala performance to mark her 90th birthday, was held at the
Theatre Royal, Haymarket, on 29 October 1972.

# Film, Radio and Television Performances

## *Film Performances*

*1921*   Mrs Brand in *Moth and Rust*

*1922*   Lady Deadlock in *Bleak House*: 'Tense Moments from Great Plays'
series (short)

*1928*   Nurse Edith Cavell in *Dawn* (Dir: Herbert Wilcox)

*1929*   The Mother in *To What Red Hell* (Dir: Edwin Greenwood)

*1931*   Mrs Hawthorn in *Hindle Wakes* (Dir: Victor Saville)

*1932*   Madame Duval in *A Gentleman of Paris* (Dir: Sinclair Hill)

*1936*   Ellen in *Tudor Rose* (Dir: Robert Stevenson)

*1941*   The General (Mrs Baines) in *Major Barbara* (Dir: Gabriel Pascal)

*1947*   Mrs Squeers in *Nicholas Nickleby* (Dir: Cavalcanti)

*1948*   Mrs Mouncey in *Britannia Mews* (Dir: Jean Negulesco)

*1950*   Mrs Gill in *Stage Fright* (Dir: Alfred Hitchcock)
Mrs Marston in *Gone to Earth* (Dir: Michael Powell and Emeric
Pressburger)

*1951*   Miss Bosanquet in *The Lady with the Lamp* (Dir: Herbert Wilcox)
The Aristocratic Client in *The Magic Box* (Dir: John Boulting)

*1953*   Queen Victoria in *Melba* (Dir: Lewis Milestone)
Mabel in *Weak and the Wicked* (Dir: J. Lee-Thompson)

*1957*   Queen Dowager in *The Prince and the Showgirl* (Dir: Laurence
Olivier)

*1958*   Dora in *Alive and Kicking* (Dir: Cyril Frankel)
Granny McKinley in *Smiley Gets a Gun* (Dir: Anthony Kimmins)

*1959*   Lady Fitzhugh in *Shake Hands with the Devil* (Dir: Michael Anderson)

*1960*   Lady Caroline in *Hand in Hand* (Dir: Philip Leacock)

## *Major Radio Performances*

1933   *Coriolanus*

1938   *A Winter's Tale*

1939   *The Persians*

       Scenes from the Tragedies of Shakespeare

1942   *Abraham and Isaac*

1944   *Jane Clegg*

       *Peer Gynt*

1945   *Henry IV*, Parts 1 and 2

1946   *The Trojan Women*

1947   *The Cenci*

       *The Blue Bird*

1948   *The White Devil*

       *Coriolanus*

       *The Corn is Green*

1949   *Brand*

1951   *Comedienne*

1952   *The Women of Troy*

1954   *Henry VIII*

1958   Scenes from Shakespeare (*Romeo and Juliet*)

1959   *The Linden Tree*

1961   *The Sunday Market*

       *A Picture of Autumn*

1962   Mystery Playhouse – *Spooner*

1963   *For Shakespeare and St George*

       *Waiting in the Wings*

1965   *God and Kate Murphy*

       *The Sacred Flame*

1966   *The Loves of Cass McGuire*

       *The Foolish Gentlewoman*

       *Jane Clegg*

1967   *The Distaff Side*

       *The Potting Shed*

       *Saint Joan*

       *A Passage to India*

       *Captain Brassbound's Conversion*

1968   *Peace*

1969   *Night Must Fall*

*The Son*
*The Captain's Log*
1971   *The Viceroy's Wife*
*Arsenic and Old Lace*
1975   *The Evening is Calm*


## Major BBC Television Performances

1959   *80 in the Shade* (Dame Sophia Carrell)
*Waters of the Moon* (Mrs Whyte)
1960   *Riders to the Sea* (Maurya)
*A Matter of Age* (Sara Champline)
1964   *The Reluctant Peer* (Dowager Countess of Lister)
1965   *A Passage to India* (Mrs Moore)

# Acknowledgements

This book began in the belief that what was missing from the shelves was not a fourth Thorndike biography but instead the first complete Thorndike chronicle: for it, therefore, I have drawn on a large number of private and public archives of reviews, press interviews, theatre histories and radio and television recordings. There are also certain individuals to whom I owe especial thanks, notably Dame Sybil's son John Casson for giving this project his blessing, her frequent director and occasional co-star Sir John Gielgud for giving it both a prologue and an epilogue, and John Curtis at Weidenfeld for giving me the chance to put the chronicle into print.

Additionally, my thanks are due to the staffs of the British Theatre Museum (Enthoven Collection), Westminster Central Reference Library, London Library, Maidenhead Library, New York Public Library (Lincoln Centre), BBC radio record and drama libraries, and above all to Raymond Mander and Joe Mitchenson without whose pictures (many in this case given to them by Dame Sybil herself) no book of mine would ever be complete.

On all of the following books I have drawn for something, be it direct quotation, indirect background material, or simply an alternative point of view against which to test certain verdicts. These then are the books that have been consciously and intentionally used while I was thinking about or writing this one, and to the author and publisher of each and every one I am most grateful. But there have been many other sources too, ranging from the reviews of dozens of theatre and film critics to the memories of countless playgoers and the interviews of more than half a hundred magazines and BBC programmes, and for those too I must express my thanks to all concerned. I am indebted also to the editor of the *Sunday Times* for allowing me to reprint Sir John Gielgud's obituary, and to the publishers and executors of the late Russell Thorndike for allowing me to reprint extracts from his sister's letters to him.

Agate, James, *Contemporary Theatre 1924* (Chapman & Hall, 1925)
              *Egos 1–9* (Harrap, 1936–48)
              *First Nights* (Nicholson & Watson, 1934)
Alpert, Hollis, *The Barrymores* (W. H. Allen, 1964)
Archer, William, *About the Theatre* (Fisher Unwin, 1886)
Bagnold, Enid, *Autobiography* (Heinemann, 1969)
Baily, Leslie, *Scrapbook for the 20s* (Muller, 1959)
Baxter, Beverley, *First Nights and Noises Off* (Hutchinson, 1949)
              *First Nights and Footlights* (Hutchinson, 1955)
Bishop, George, *My Betters* (Heinemann, 1957)
Brown, Ivor, *Theatre 1 & 2* (Max Reinhardt, 1955, 1956)
              *Old and Young* (Bodley Head, 1971)
Burton, Hal (ed.), *Great Acting* (BBC Publications, 1967)
Casson, John, *Lewis and Sybil* (Collins, 1972)
Cochran, Charles B., *Secrets of a Showman* (Heinemann, 1935)
Cottrell, John *Laurence Olivier* (Weidenfeld & Nicolson, 1975)
Craig, Edward, *Gordon Craig* (Gollancz, 1968)
Darlington, W. A., *6001 Nights* (Harrap, 1960)
Dean, Basil, *Seven Ages* (Hutchinson, 1970)
           *Mind's Eye* (Hutchinson, 1973)
Driberg, Tom, *Swaff* (Macdonald, 1974)
Findlater, Richard, *The Unholy Trade* (Gollancz, 1953)
             *Emlyn Williams* (Rockliff, 1956)
             *Banned!* (MacGibbon & Kee, 1967)
             *Lilian Baylis* (Allen Lane, 1975)
             *The Player Queens* (Weidenfeld & Nicolson, 1976)
Forsyth, James, *Tyrone Guthrie* (Hamish Hamilton, 1976)
Gaye, Freda (ed.), *Who's Who in the Theatre*, 14th ed. (Pitman, 1967)
Gielgud, John, *Early Stages* (Macmillan, 1939)
             *Distinguished Company* (Heinemann, 1972)
Gifford, Denis, *British Film Catalogue 1895–1970* (David & Charles, 1973)
Gourlay, Logan, *Laurence Olivier* (Weidenfeld & Nicolson, 1973)
Guthrie, Tyrone, *A Life in the Theatre* (Hamish Hamilton, 1959)
             *On Acting* (Studio Vista, 1971)
Haddon, Archibald, *Green Room Gossip* (Stanley Paul, 1922)
             *Hallo Playgoers* (Cecil Palmer, 1924)
Halliwell, Leslie, *The Filmgoer's Companion* (Hart-Davis MacGibbon, 1974)
Harwood, Ronald, *Donald Wolfit* (Secker, 1971)

Hayman, Ronald, *John Gielgud* (Heinemann, 1971)

Herbert, Ian (ed.), *Who's Who in the Theatre*, 16th ed. (Pitman, 1977)

Hobson, Harold, *Theatre 1 & 2* (Longmans, 1948, 1950)

      *Ralph Richardson* (Rockliff, 1958)

Johns, Eric, *Dames of the Theatre* (W. H. Allen, 1974)

Keown, Eric, *Peggy Ashcroft* (Rockliff, 1955)

Loraine, Winifred, *Robert Loraine* (Collins, 1938)

Low, Rachael, *History of British Films 1918–29* (Allen & Unwin, 1971)

MacQueen Pope, W., *Ghosts and Greasepaint* (Robert Hale, 1951)

      *The Footlights Flickered* (Jenkins, 1959)

Mander, Raymond, and Mitchenson, Joe, *Theatrical Companion to Shaw* (Rockliff, 1954)

Morley, Robert, and Stokes, Sewell, *Responsible Gentleman* (Heinemann, 1966)

Nicholson, Nora, *Chameleon's Dish* (Elek, 1973)

Parker, John (ed.), *Who's Who in the Theatre*, eds 1–13 (Pitman, 1912–61)

Patch, Blanche, *Thirty Years with GBS* (Gollancz, 1951)

Perry, George, *The Great British Picture Show* (Hart-Davis MacGibbon, 1974)

Prideaux, Tom, *Love or Nothing* (Millington, 1975)

Roberts, Peter, *The Old Vic Story* (W. H. Allen, 1976)

Speaight, Robert, *Shakespeare on the Stage* (Collins, 1973)

Sprigge, Elizabeth, *Sybil Thorndike Casson* (Gollancz, 1971)

Stephens, Frances (ed), *Theatre World Annuals 1–10* (Rockliff, 1950–60)

Taylor, John Russell, *The Rise and Fall of the Well-Made Play* (Methuen, 1967)

*Theatre Arts Anthology* (Theatre Arts Books, New York, 1950)

Thorndike, Russell, *Sybil Thorndike* (Thornton Butterworth, 1929)

Thorndike, Russell and Sybil, *Lilian Baylis* (Chapman Hall, 1938)

Trewin, J. C., *Theatre Programme* (Muller, 1954)

     *Edith Evans* (Rockliff, 1954)

     *Sybil Thorndike* (Rockliff, 1955)

     *Paul Scofield* (Rockliff, 1956)

     *The Gay Twenties* (Macdonald, 1958)

     *The Turbulent Thirties* (Macdonald, 1960)

     *Robert Donat* (Heinemann, 1968)

Tynan, Kenneth, *He That Plays The King* (Longmans, 1950)

     *Curtains* (Longmans, 1961)

     *Tynan Right and Left* (Longmans, 1967)

Van Thal, Herbert (ed.), *An Agate Anthology* (Hart-Davis, 1961)
Webster, Margaret, *The Same Only Different* (Gollancz, 1969)
Williams, Emlyn, *George* (Hamish Hamilton, 1961)
       *Emlyn* (Bodley Head, 1973)
Williams, Neville, *Chronology of the Modern World* (Barrie & Rockliff, 1966)
Williamson, Audrey, *Theatre of Two Decades* (Rockliff, 1951)
       *Old Vic Drama 1 & 2* (Rockliff, 1948, 1957)
Wilson, A. E., *Playgoer's Pilgrimage* (Stanley Paul, undated)

For the major part of the list of stage performances, I am most grateful to Barrie & Jenkins Ltd and to J. C. Trewin in whose Thorndike monograph it first appeared in 1955.

The publisher and I would like to thank the following persons and organizations for permission to reproduce copyright material: Houston Rogers: 13, 123 (*above*), 139 (*above*); Mander and Mitchenson: 21 (*above and below*), 24, 35 (*above and below*), 47, 61 (*above left, above right, below*), 65 (*above*), 71 (*above left, above right, below*), 79 (*above and below*), 81, 85 (*above, below left, below right*), 97 (*above and below*), 99 (*below*), 103, 109 (*above and below*), 127 (*above*); Victoria & Albert Museum, Enthoven Collection: 65 (*below*), 77, 87 (*below*); Mansell Collection: 69 (*above left, below left, right*); Radio Times Hulton Picture Library: 87 (*above*), 105 (*above and below*), 119 (*below*); Kobal Collection: 93 (*above*), 129 (*below*), 135 (*above*); Popperfoto: 93 (*below*), 145; Ronald Grant Collections: 99 (*above*), 123 (*below*), 135 (*below*); John Vickers: 115, 117, 119 (*above*); Angus McBean, Tennent: 125, 127 (*below*), 129 (*above*); David Fairweather, Chichester Festival Theatre: 137; Thorndike Theatre, Leatherhead: 139 (*below*), 141 (*above and below*)

# Index

Page numbers in *italic* refer to the illustrations